"I have had the joy of meeting Paul Borthwick in a variety of places around the world. Like in previous books he has published, in this one he shows the ability to put a lot of information in a readable and meaningful way. Going through the second part of this book, it is evident that Paul wants people to change and grow as persons, and to this end he puts together missionary passion, pastoral savvy and good readable style."

Samuel Escobar, Valencia, Spain, professor emeritus of missiology, Palmer Theological Seminary, professor, the Facultad Protestante de Teología UEBE, Madrid, author, *The New Global Mission*

"Borthwick has done it again! He has provided us with a thoughtful and provocative analysis of the world as well as challenging Christians to think about their opportunities and responsibilities for global engagement. As both a product of and leader in the short-term mission movement for many years, I now see the world differently. While very grateful for my 'missions' experiences, I am now compelled to see through the eyes of our global family, 92% of which lives outside North America. The kinds of questions that Borthwick raises are very similar to the issues on my mind. I think this book should be required reading for all short-termers and church leaders who want to make a global impact."

Dr. Geoff Tunnicliffe, chief executive officer/secretary general, World Evangelical Alliance

"This book is exceptional! Paul truly gets at the issues that are most critical for people in North America to understand if they hope to fruitfully engage in global mission. I will be recommending this book to many people! It should be required reading for any pastor, layperson or missionary who has not recently engaged in significant missiological research. It is an excellent tool to help North Americans get up to speed on what God is doing in the world and how they need to adapt if they desire to be a blessing and not a hindrance to his purposes."

Mary Lederleitner, missionary-in-residence, Wheaton College, crosscultural consultant, Wycliffe Global Alliance, and author, *Cross-Cultural Partnerships*

"*Western Christians in Global Mission* combines up-to-date analysis of what God is doing worldwide with passionate commitment to obeying and fulfilling the Great Commission. Here is a textbook for students, a guidebook for missions leaders, a study book for small groups and a challenge book for every Christian."

Leith Anderson, president, National Association of Evangelicals, Washington, DC

"Get ready for some tough questions and humbling stories! Borthwick brilliantly gathers voices from around the globe and paints an honest picture of the North American church in global missions. This book is a must-read for anyone wanting to gain a 10,000-foot view of our changing world or wanting to build effective partnerships with Majority World churches."

Tom Lin, vice president, director of missions and director of the
Urbana Student Missions Conference, InterVarsity Christian Fellowship/USA

"It's easy to hang our heads in despair over the many ills of Western missions. But many of us stop there, paralyzed from doing anything. In typical Borthwick style, Paul draws upon his vast experiences to suggest solutions for how we can and should engage in global mission for such a time as this."

David Livermore, Ph.D., author of *Serving with Eyes Wide Open* and
Leading with Cultural Intelligence

"Paul vividly paints a picture of just how our globalized world has so dramatically changed and what that means for us in the West. The key question of the West's role in a new nonwhite, nonwealthy and non-Western world is a pressing one for the church in the U.S. but one that few have the ability or courage to press into. Paul invites us into both a journey in understanding the world around us and a journey into the soul of the church, carefully navigating complex issues so the rest of us can benefit from a life of dedication to mission. As a missiological work, Paul's contribution to this growing body of literature is indispensable for churches historically committed to mission but now wondering what role, if any, the church in the U.S. can play. I highly recommend this book!"

R. York Moore, national evangelist, InterVarsity Christian Fellowship/USA,
author of *Making All Things New*

"Today's huge changes in the world and the church are bewildering to navigate. How can we be part of what God has called all believers to be and do—his witnesses in a hurting and needy world? Paul Borthwick's analysis of the global church comes from his friendships with many in the Majority World. Writing as a reflective practitioner, Paul helps Western Christians face critical issues of attitude, heart and strategy with grace, courage, cross-cultural sensitivity and a learner's heart. This book presents a strong, clear invitation to missional living. It will help you align yourself and your church with what God is doing in his world today."

Jeanette Yep, pastor of regional and global outreach, Grace Chapel,
Lexington, Massachusetts

WESTERN CHRISTIANS IN GLOBAL MISSION

What's the Role of the North American Church?

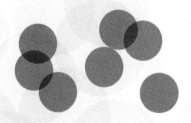

PAUL BORTHWICK

FOREWORD BY FEMI B. ADELEYE

IVP Books

An imprint of InterVarsity Press
Downers Grove, Illinois

InterVarsity Press
P.O. Box 1400, Downers Grove, IL 60515-1426
World Wide Web: www.ivpress.com
E-mail: email@ivpress.com

InterVarsity Press® is the book-publishing division of InterVarsity Christian Fellowship/USA®, a
movement of students and faculty active on campus at hundreds of universities, colleges and schools of
nursing in the United States of America, and a member movement of the International Fellowship of
Evangelical Students. For information about local and regional activities, write Public Relations Dept.,
InterVarsity Christian Fellowship/USA, 6400 Schroeder Rd., P.O. Box 7895, Madison, WI 53707-7895, or
visit the IVCF website at <www.intervarsity.org>.

All Scripture quotations, unless otherwise indicated, are taken from THE HOLY BIBLE, NEW
INTERNATIONAL VERSION®. NIV®. Copyright ©1973, 1978, 1984, 2011 by Biblica, Inc.™ Used by
permission. All rights reserved worldwide.

While all stories in this book are true, some names and identifying information in this book have been
changed to protect the privacy of the individuals involved.

Cover design: Cindy Kiple
Images: JurgaR/Getty Images
Interior design: Beth Hagenberg

ISBN 978-0-8308-3780-9

Printed in the United States of America ∞

Library of Congress Cataloging-in-Publication Data has been requested.

P	18	17	16	15	14	13	12	11	10	9	8	7	6	5	4	3	2	1
Y	27	26	25	24	23	22	21	20	19	18	17	16	15	14	13	12

Contents

Foreword

Paul Borthwick has invited us to undertake a journey together. He writes as one who knows God's world as well as ours. He understands our collective world enough to challenge us to give up our comfort zones or our inclination to succumb to a withdrawal syndrome, which suggests that "because the Christian center of gravity and of missionary involvement has shifted, what else is there for some of us to do?" This is mission as well as theology brewed not in an ivory tower but where the rubber meets the road in the context of real-life struggles and power encounters. In addition to his own travels and experiences Paul has cited various other people whose lives and works provide a deep understanding of the changing nature of God's world.

Yes, Paul demonstrates in this book that the world has changed significantly from what it was when pioneer missionaries first went out. Nevertheless it is as much God's world today as it was then. Let us never imagine that the fast-paced globalized nature of a technology-driven world would fill the vacuum or emptiness of the human heart.

The stress on the shift in Christian gravity has in some contexts produced at least three unhelpful responses. One suggests that God has finished with some parts of the world. Another suggests that since the center of mission-sending agencies has also shifted to previous recipients, those from previous sending territories can rest from our labors or take a vacation. A third suggests that newly arrived missionaries lack the historical heritage of ownership, so how competent are they?

The first response is as much a misunderstanding of God as it is a dangerous misconception. God neither gives up nor leaves himself without a witness in any part of his world. The second underestimates the need for all hands to be on deck with the harnessing of all God's gifts to us in our diversity to hasten the task before us. If indeed we are on the last lap in our expectation of the King's return, this is no time for anyone to relax or withdraw because others are involved. Rather it is a time to persevere in finishing the race together. The third response forgets that the Lord of the Harvest is sovereign enough to send whomever he pleases from anywhere to anywhere. In place of such responses, Paul suggests that we learn as much as possible about realities of God's world and work, take them seriously and align ourselves with the diverse ways God has worked in and through various people in different parts of his world.

Paul has exercised tough love, particularly in addressing issues Christians in the Global North must contend with and in nudging us all to explore what Christ would do as represented in the accounts of real people he has encountered and brought into this journey. But we must not assume that this book is for Americans or Christians in the Global North alone. It is for us all—members of God's world and family, preordained to be born in different locations of his world according to his plan and purposes (Acts 17:26-28). He has in his wisdom given us diverse gifts to make a difference in our "Jerusalem" and wherever he sends us.

Let those who talk of taking the gospel "back to sender" look at their backyard and be reminded that the task is not necessarily finished there. We all know that it is by grace that we have been saved. It is as much by grace that we can meaningfully and relevantly serve

God's purposes together in global missions. This journey should be a journey together, bearing in mind that, as the East African Revivalists used to say, "at the foot of the cross, the ground is equal."

I share Paul's concern about "short term" mission experiences. We need to balance this with the perspective that our pioneers actually carried their belongings in caskets, some fully expecting to be the luggage on the return journey—if there was to be one.

The journey Paul calls us to undertake in and through this book is worth embracing! I've had the privilege of spending time with Paul, in Kenya, Zimbabwe, South Africa, Germany, Nigeria and the United States, and found him at home in each of those contexts.

Enjoy the journey!

Femi B. Adeleye
Akropong, Ghana

Preface

An Invitation to a Journey

This book is an invitation to join me on a journey into global Christianity, a family of followers of Jesus Christ from almost every corner of the earth. It's an invitation to discover new relationships with a family that worships in over two thousand languages and arguably represents the most ethnically, geographically and economically diverse religious grouping the world has ever known. It's an invitation to explore what God is doing in the world and an invitation to discover afresh where we fit in God's overall global plan: his *mission*.

We join this journey at different phases of life, and we come from a variety of experiences related to the global church. Some readers are young and are just getting started on the journey. Our curiosity about the world has been stimulated by a college friend from China or a coworker from India. Others have already experienced a taste of the global, multicultural church by serving on a short-term mission trip to Mexico or Haiti. Fascination with what we saw or learned has left us yearning to know more. Still others have spent a semester overseas, served the poor in an urban slum or rescued people from human trafficking. These isolated experiences have created a desire to know more of the big picture.

Older readers like me may have been involved for a very long time. We find ourselves a little dizzy with all of the changes in the world: from governments to economics to the growth and significance of the non-Western, Majority World church.

Where do we fit in this globalized church?

I intentionally use the word *journey* because we are on the road to an amazing, multicultural destination, with worshipers from every people, nation, tribe and language. The apostle John paints a picture of this for us in Revelation 5:9 and 7:9. But the exact map for this journey is not always clear. As a result—and I say this as a warning to readers—I raise as many questions as I answer as we ponder the road ahead. In short, if you are looking for a nice, tidy roadmap into our globalized future, this book will leave you disappointed.

My Journey

My first glimpse into the world of global Christianity came as a result of my Christian parents. International visitors, my dad's World War II stories, prayers for the global church and physical symbols of a world beyond my white, middle-class neighborhood (such as maps, coins and stamps) provoked in me a desire for travel and adventure. As a child, I wanted to explore exotic places like Upper Volta (now Burkina Faso) or visit the islands of the Philippines or smuggle Bibles into the Soviet Union.

In college, I started reading missionary biographies. Elisabeth Elliot's accounts of her husband Jim's story, contained in *Shadow of the Almighty* and *Through Gates of Splendor*, challenged me to a higher level of devotion to Christ. Hudson Taylor's *Spiritual Secret* introduced me to a deeper life of faith and trust, and the story of Adoniram and Ann Judson exemplified lives of sacrifice.

In 1973, when I was nineteen, I attended the Urbana Missions Conference, which opened my eyes to a global God with a global calling into a global world of need. But all my learning was fundamentally cognitive, not experiential. When I was twenty-four, a ministry trip to Haiti launched me into a global adventure unlike I could have ever imagined. My first-ever plane flight, combined with my first-ever trip out of the United States, combined with my first-ever exposure to the Majority World: these things shaped the entire direction of my life after that point.[1]

Within months, my girlfriend, Christie, and I were leading a team of fourteen high school students on a work project to Cartagena, Colombia. Over the next two decades, as a youth pastor and later a global mission pastor, I, along with Christie, who became my wife in 1979, coordinated over one hundred of these short-term mission teams, mostly to Majority World destinations as diverse as Kenya, Trinidad, Morocco, Surinam, Zambia and Peru.

I look at these short-term mission trips now with a more critical eye, and some of my concerns about the short-term mission phenomenon will appear throughout this book. In reality, we were really more spectators and learners—*voluntourists,* in the most positive light, or *poverty voyeurs,* in the most negative—rather than positive contributors to the long-term growth of the church. Nevertheless, by the grace of God, short-term missions introduced us to relationships with

- believers in Haiti, who exuded a spiritual joy in spite of abject poverty, unjust governments and what was for us unimaginable hardship

- believers in Colombia, whose hospitality gave us a sense of belonging to a global family much larger than we knew at home

- believers in Morocco, who faced opposition unlike anything we knew

- peoples and cultures dominated by the other great world religions—Islam, Hinduism and Buddhism

- people who talked openly about supernatural signs, wonders, miracles, demons and spiritual warfare

- Christians whose zeal for evangelizing exposed an absence of that zeal in the church in our own country

In spite of all the good learning and the initiation of global friendships, we were still American-centric in our worldviews. We were still convinced that the church in North America was the leader in global Christianity and that the rest of the world was our mission target.[2] Our global Christianity paradigm assumed that the gospel would go "from the West to the rest." We had the resources; they were the poor. We were the missionaries; they were the recipients of our courageous efforts. The real needs were "out there" somewhere, and we were the messengers of hope.

Everything changed for us at a conference in 1987 called Singapore 87: A Conference of Younger Leaders. We were honored to be invited to a conference with more than three hundred participants from more than sixty countries, most of whom were from the Majority World. We went to that conference flush with confidence. We represented a globally minded congregation with a rich mission history and a mission budget approaching one million dollars. We were feeling pretty full of ourselves and our American-influenced, financially backed lives. We expected to hear at that conference about how the United States church would lead the way toward the twenty-first century and beyond.

Instead, God used that conference to turn our global church perspective upside down. Todd Johnson of the Center for the Study of Global Christianity says that for North Americans to be effectively involved in the Majority World church, there must be a reorientation of our thinking.[3] Singapore 87 was the beginning of our worldview reorientation. We met leaders from Nigeria and India who were training and sending missionaries from their own countries. We were taught through the preaching and testimonies of Christians from Sri Lanka, Nepal, Kenya, Poland and the Middle East. We heard phrases like "the church going from everywhere to anywhere," and "the whole church takes the whole gospel to the whole world."

I remember one worship experience in which we were all singing "Our God Reigns." One of the verses begins, "How lovely on the mountains are the feet of him who brings good news." I was standing next to the only Nepali delegate to the conference. His coworker had been arrested for his faith the day before he was to fly to join us. In his cultural tradition, the man next to me worshiped barefoot (as in God's command to Moses in Exodus 3:5 to take off his sandals, because he was standing on holy ground). As we sang about the feet bringing good news across the mountains, I saw my brother's feet. I thought about the thousands of Hindu villages scattered across mountainous Nepal, and I realized we were singing about his feet: feet that were taking the gospel to places I will never see. I confessed, "Lord, you are doing something in the world I never knew."

We went to the conference expecting to hear how the church in North America was leading the global church into the new millennium. In contrast, we left the conference praying, "Lord, please don't leave the church in North America behind as you move powerfully into the world."

Since that time, our lives have been more about joining the work of God in the world than leading the way. In language made familiar through Henry Blackaby's writings, we are looking for where God is going and joining him.[4]

When I served as a global outreach pastor, Christie and I started developing relationships and partnerships with global colleagues. Opportunities to minister with the brothers and sisters we met at the conference took us and our church to Sri Lanka, Uganda, Egypt, Pakistan, India, Croatia and Ecuador. Over time, we developed relationships with Christian brothers and sisters named Femi, Affiong, Ajith, Nelun, Yacoub, Funmi, Fayez, Ubaldo, Jorge, Kwabena, Suleyman and more. These family members have become our teachers, our coworkers and, in some cases, deep friends.

When we sensed God was leading us more into full-time global ministry, we joined a group dedicated to working alongside of and under the direction of Majority World church leaders. We went from inviting leaders in the Majority World to join us in fulfilling our vision to asking Majority World leaders if we had anything to offer them that could help them fulfill their vision.

As we embark on this journey, I'm pleased to tell you that God is not leaving the church in North America behind. In his global mission, there are plenty of places to join with a global family to be part of what God is doing in the world. This is the theme of this book: finding our place as members of the family of God from North America serving alongside our global family.

Questions and Next Steps

1. Where are you on the journey into the global church?

2. Who can you join with to start discussing the ideas of this book so that your journey into the world becomes a team effort?

3. One of the big ideas of this book is building relationships. Do you have any early ideas of how, starting with your existing network of connections, you might become more connected to the Majority World church?

Introduction

Questions for the Journey

What should North American Christians' involvement and identity in the global church be? How can we who are globally involved and interested wrestle with questions related to the growth of the church in the Majority World? And how does this global awareness combine with the decline of Christianity in the post-Christian West and the corresponding Western loss of confidence in the gospel?

Some estimate that 70 percent of the world's Bible-believing Christians (as opposed to nominal or cultural Christians) now live in the Majority World.[1] If we are aware of the growth of the church in the world, and if we are aware of missionary-sending endeavors from places like South Korea, India, Nigeria, Brazil and China, we will logically begin asking questions like:

- What is the role of the North American church in global Christianity?

- Is there a place for us in God's global plan, and if so, where? And what do we have to offer?

- When people think that the work of global mission has passed to the Majority World, what are the future challenges of mobilizing the church in North America?

- How does all of this relate to the ethnic minority church plants across North America, which are filled with those who have emigrated here?

- Do we believe there is a place for us? More importantly, does the Majority World church believe there is a place for us?

- What perspectives and paradigms do we need to change?

- How can we be involved financially without creating paternalism from the North American church or dependency in the Majority World church?

This book will explore these big-picture questions. I hope to raise the issues that can help us develop full involvement in the global purposes of God, in ways relevant to the realities of the global church. If you are looking for a resource on "planning global strategies," this book is probably not it.[2] The only "strategies" for global mission that I present here are based on relationships and servant leadership.

Three Contrasting Perspectives

In my travels and research, I have observed three primary ways North American Christians interact with the global church. These observations are overgeneralized, but they help set the broad parameters of the challenge facing us as North American Christians.

Globally aware young Christians. First, there is the perspective of globally aware young people. They have grown up in an information-rich world where they have been encouraged to embrace multiculturalism, fight for justice-related issues and expand their global understanding. These globally informed younger adults want involvement in the global church through relationships. They are often more willing to serve under national leadership, take risks in standing for justice and dive into crosscultural experiences.

Although globally aware, these young adults seem unclear on what the gospel is beyond just "doing good." In spite of the fact that these younger people align themselves with Christian faith, they shy away from wrestling with issues of theology and missiology, especially regarding the matter of the uniqueness and exclusivity of Jesus Christ as the only way of salvation.

They love the tangible expression of Christian faith, but most of their theology and practice focus on the acting out of the gospel here and now and speaking to the current needs in this world. Start talking about life after death, heaven and hell, eternal judgment and salvation, and they either respond with uncertainty or reject these ideas as the preoccupations of a previous generation, whose gospel was too focused on the next life and not enough on the needs now.

In spite of the desire for relational connectivity, the greatest ministry challenge facing these younger Christians is arguably long-term commitment. In their fast-moving, ever-changing world, concentration on any one thing for more than three or six months is very challenging. Going on a short-term mission trip to rescue people from human trafficking is one thing; investing years or decades in fighting unjust legal systems is another.

Locally focused Christians. A second group of Christians have taken the growth of the global church as a reason to focus only on local realities. They may think that North American Christians are no longer needed beyond our own borders. Kirk Franklin, international president of the Wycliffe Bible Translators, writes that the U.S. church is hearing messages like "send more money, not people" or "Christian nationals can do it better, faster and cheaper."[3] This has led to a diminishing interest in North America in the global mission of the church. Or perhaps they think that "needs here at home" should dominate our efforts. As one church leader told me, "Let's fix America first." From his perspective, global outreach must wait until we get our own house in order.

In one respect, he has a good point, as the church in Europe reminds us. The decline of Christianity in Western Europe was often overlooked because of the "over-there" focus of the mission community.[4] In reality, however, some Christians use the "needs here at home" as a smokescreen to cover their uncertainty about the uniqueness of Jesus as the one and only Savior in our pluralistic world.[5] Building off of the unfortunate realities of Christian mission's historic association with colonialism and imperialism, these believers want to shy away from proclaiming Jesus alone as Savior.

American-centric Christians. A third perspective features those who are convinced of the uniqueness of Christ and are desirous to go into all the world, but whose view of the global church is still very North American–centric. These Christians still hold the "from the West to the rest" worldview.

Timothy Tennent writes about this when he refers to "the collapse of the 'West Reaches the Rest' paradigm." He notes that "Western Christians have been slow to grasp the full missiological implications of the simultaneous expansion and emergence of a post-Christian West and a post-Western Christianity: the church worldwide fulfilling the missiological task."[6] Tennent is referring to "business as usual" churches, mission agencies and missions enthusiasts whose paradigm for mission strategy and relationships with national believers looks more like the 1970s than the twenty-first century. The "business as usual" agency has a board made up of white, middle-aged or older males working with a "from us to them" attitude. The "business as usual" church supports crosscultural missionaries, but these folks are all the same culture and ethnicity of the majority of the members of the church.

I had a sad encounter with this "business as usual" paradigm on my second trip to the Murtala Muhammed International Airport in Lagos, Nigeria. In 2002, the U.S. State Department warned Americans against travel to Lagos, so if there were other Americans on the flight, they were oil company workers, USAID workers or missionaries.

As I stood at baggage claim, an American couple asked me where I was headed and why I was in Lagos. I explained that I was on my way to Ibadan, a large city north of Lagos. They explained that they were working in Ibadan as missionaries.

They asked how I was getting to the city, and I explained that my Nigerian hosts were picking me up. When they asked what mission I was with (meaning which North American agency), they were visibly shocked to realize that I was there only to work with Nigerians. "We chose Ibadan because we know there are no gospel-preaching churches in Ibadan," they explained. "Why are you going there?"

I found their comment surprising, because I had been to Ibadan the year before and every street sign seemed to have the name of five or six churches posted on it. I remember reading the names like "Glory Tabernacle," "Divine Healing Center," "Fire from Heaven Miracle Center," "Full Stature in Christ Church" and "Evangelical Church Winning All."

I responded, "I'm speaking at a mission conference for Full Stature Mission, where they are expecting more than one thousand Ibadan pastors representing more than two hundred ministries." At this point, I think my American colleagues must have deemed me a religious heretic. How could I be speaking to one thousand pastors in a city that had "no gospel-preaching churches"?

Our conversation revealed the differences between their paradigm and mine. They were sent by a U.S.-based ministry that defined "gospel-preaching churches" as non-Pentecostal and noncharismatic, male-led, emotionally quiet, hymn-singing and (implicitly) led by white missionaries. My paradigm was more along the lines of "go where God is going."

All of us have different responses to the realities of the changing global church. I pray that the stories and ideas that follow will help us all move where God is going.

As You Start This Book

My passion is to challenge readers, no matter what our perspective, that our global involvement is not built on current trends or on a pluralistic environment but rather on the biblical global mandate.

The biblical mandate, combined with the stewardship of the amazing human and material resources of North America, compel us to find our fit. The way that we join forces with the Majority World church is new and different, but we need to find ways to say yes to God's invitation to grow with our global family. We need to remember that the biblical mandates for global involvement stand today for all Christians everywhere.

- "Declare his glory among the nations, his marvelous deeds among all peoples" (Ps 96:3).
- "Make disciples of all nations" (Mt 28:19).
- "Preach the good news to all creation" (Mk 16:15).
- "You will be my witnesses in Jerusalem, and in all Judea and Samaria, and to the ends of the earth" (Acts 1:8).

Whether you're a globally aware student, a church leader responsible for global outreach, a preparing missionary, a church pastor desirous of enlarging your congregation's world vision or a worker in a Christian mission agency, I hope that this book gives you new insights and ideas on connecting your local life to the global purposes of God.

The book has two primary sections. The first part is dedicated to a current analysis of the world, the church in North America and the church in the Majority World. Part two, the lengthier section, then offers ideas for moving forward. This second section will attempt to synthesize global realities with local responses so that we can move forward in international relationships and crosscultural involvement.

Questions and Next Steps

1. What has shaped your view of the world and our Christian response in it? Where do you find yourself in the three perspectives?

    (a) Globally aware but unclear on how to integrate your faith?

    (b) Thinking that global mission is no longer our North American responsibility (we need to focus here at home and let the Majority World church do the work of missions)?

    (c) Desirous of old paradigms in which we see ourselves as in the global mission driver's seat?

2. What are you reading (besides this book) to expand your global vision?

Part One

Where Are We Now?

How do we understand our world, our churches in North America and churches in the Majority World? I am acutely aware that assuming that I can do justice to any of these three realities in a few short pages is presumptuous. Nevertheless, I hope to identify issues and raise questions which will help us understand where we are, so that we can prepare for the way forward. Like the Old Testament men of Issachar, we want to understand our times so that we can direct the responses of the church of Jesus Christ (1 Chron 12:32). In the words of John Stott, we want to be able to understand both God's *Word* and the *world* into which he sends us.[1]

Given this fast-paced, ever-changing world, we can easily fail to take note of these changes with respect to our faith. On a global scale, we are living with the fruits of the labors and the sacrifices of people who, over the last two hundred years, gave their lives to spread the gospel around the world.

At one conference in Accra, Ghana, dedicated to challenging university students to get involved in global mission, leaders referred three or four times to the history of the European missionaries who came to Ghana in the nineteenth century. They came with their earthly belongings packed in their own coffins, because they knew they would die there. Some 60 percent of these pioneers died in their first two years of service in Ghana, but they planted the seed of the gospel. The conference leaders wanted to remind these students that they were the fruit of those missionary's sacrifice.

In spite of all the mistakes that missionaries made over the years, the spread of God's kingdom has been unstoppable. In the 1880s, there was scarcely a Christian in Korea. Missionaries went there, shared the gospel and empowered the church with the concept that they could be self-supporting, self-governing and self-propagating. Now South Korea is the second largest missionary-sending country in the world.

The continent of Africa in 1910 was 9.4 percent Christian, with an estimated 11.7 million people identifying themselves as Christian. By the year 2010, the estimate was that the continent is now 48 percent Christian, with 495 million Christian believers.[2] By the year 2025, some estimate that Africa will be home to 1.031 billion believers.[3]

We need to celebrate, but we also need to remember how we got here.[4] The gospel message has been taken into the world by common people like you and me, who were willing to enter other cultures and live with the people. This has been called *incarnational living*, following the example of Jesus in John 1:14. It has been carried by people willing to learn languages, patiently endure and sacrifice—in many of the earliest cases, to the point of death—so that every person would have the opportunity to hear the invitation to come into a relationship with the living God through Jesus Christ.

Five Introductory Statements

Let me start with five statements about this globalized world. I will go into greater details with some of these statements later, but for now these will lay out some of the global realities that the church is facing. Some of these ideas (including trends like the migrations of people and the rich-poor divide) will appear again in chapter one, but my emphasis is intentional. Expressing and underscoring some of these dramatic changes in our world can serve to heighten our awareness and challenge our responses.

Young, restless, uncertain. First, our world is young, restless and uncertain. More than 50 percent of the world is under the age of twenty-five. China has more teenagers than the U.S. has people. In some of the countries in the Middle East, more than 50 percent of the population is under fourteen years old. When we look at the demographics of North America, we don't necessarily realize this, because we see our world as getting older and greyer. Churches are planning ahead more for ministry to the geriatric populations rather than to teenagers. But the reality is that most of the world is getting younger.

When I say *restless*, I'm thinking of youth-driven movements of protest against unjust governments or unfair labor practices or the ever-present rich-poor gap. The message seems to be, "We don't know what we want, but we know we don't want what we've got." The zealous youth of the world want change, but they're not sure what they want to change to.

As we ask, "Where do we fit in this globalized world and church?" consider student ministry. Working with those under age twenty-five is significant, because this is the time when young people shape their worldviews. It's the time when they decide not only what kind of world they want to enter but what kind of world they want to help create. They are young, restless and uncertain.

In response to this young world, the global family of followers of Jesus Christ must enter with the message of hope. The hope we speak of must be tangible, touching areas like unemployment, education and societal structures so that young people truly have freedom to dream. There is a saying in the Middle East that "poverty is the mother of terrorism." And hopelessness is the mother of a lot of violence in the world. If the choice is between going to a great banquet in heaven with seventy virgins versus living a life of unemployment and poverty, some will be willing to blow themselves up to escape this life.

Nonwhite, non-Western, nonwealthy. Second, our Christian family is nonwhite, non-Western and nonwealthy. Tim Tennent explains that the growth of the Majority World church has resulted in the "simultaneous emergence of multiple new centers of Christian vitality which has created a multidirectional mission with six sending and receiving continents."[5]

We can sit at home in North America and celebrate the non-Western growth of the church, but if we want to be involved, we will face some great challenges in downsizing our North American expectations and our sense of entitlements. How can we work with our global brothers and sisters to spread the gospel in places that are politically violent, economically poor and sociologically very difficult for any North American?

When I say *nonwhite* and *nonwealthy*, I am suggesting that our faith is both being molded by and molding the diverse cultures of the world. Christian faith is being molded by those cultures: there's an Indian cultural component in Indian Christianity, and there is an African component in African Christians' worship styles and their view of ancestors. But Christianity is also helping to shape these cultures. Chinese scholars are studying the relationship of Christianity to the prosperity of North American culture, and the president of Burundi has been known to bring a church choir with him as he travels.[6]

Those of us who want to interact globally will have to suspend some of our theological judgments and listen to how someone from another land is hearing the Scriptures, experiencing the power of God or applying the Bible to daily life. Mark Noll of Notre Dame writes in this regard: "In the last one hundred years, the course of evangelical Christianity has been accelerated and complicated by two notable developments: first, the rise of Pentecostal or charismatic expressions of the faith and, second, the rise of indigenous Christian churches . . . that are essentially independent."[7]

Nonwhite, non-Western and nonwealthy: our faith has to go hand in hand with poverty alleviation. The places where the gospel is growing fastest are also some of the poorest places. Most of us in North America are living on an island of affluence in the sea of poverty. We fail to realize this, because we think that everyone else around us is more affluent. So we often think of ourselves as "poor," failing to remember our relative position in this globalized world.

Missiologist Andrew Walls writes that the Majority World church will be "a Church of the poor. Christianity will be mainly the religion of rather poor and very poor people with few gifts to bring except the gospel itself. And the heartlands of the Church will include some of the poorest countries on earth."[8]

Technologized and lonely. Our world is more connected than ever and maybe more superficial than ever. I have more than two thousand Facebook friends. Do any of them know my wife's birthday? Or *my* birthday? (Without looking at my Facebook information, that is.) What kind of friends are they?

A youth pastor in Toronto argued with me that our Facebook friends *are* our genuine close friends. I didn't know how to respond. Has virtuality replaced reality? We live in a world with increasing numbers of what I call "high five" relationships. Technology has introduced us to a world where we're just going through *like, like, like, liking* each other—that's a Facebook analogy, in case you didn't get it—but sacrificing relationships of substance.

Involvement in the global church will call us back to building genuine, trusting, interdependent friendships. Our sisters and brothers around the world are generally more relational than we are, and our lives will be enriched by their hospitality and love. But we must remember, as one Christian from India told me, "You don't make friends by texting."

Conflicted about faith. Fourth, we're living in a world of faith and conflict. I'm over fifty years old. When I was in high school and college, "world religions" (with the exception of a few neighbors of the Jewish faith) referred to some exotic belief system with unusual traditions in a place across an ocean. We could read facts and objective statements about other faiths without actually knowing anyone of another faith. The migration of peoples has ended that kind of worldview. Now the Hindu is my neighbor, the Buddhist is my coworker and the Muslim is my medical doctor. Sports heroes convert to Islam, the guy who owns the supermarket is from the Sikh faith and movie stars follow the Dalai Lama of Tibetan Buddhism.

These personal relationships make it more difficult to make generalized statements about who is in "spiritual darkness" and who is not, especially when many of our neighbors are nicer and more moral than some who call themselves Christian. Therefore, many North Americans, even those who call themselves followers of Jesus, conclude that all religions are fundamentally the same. Stephen Prothero's *God Is Not One: The Eight Rival Religions That Run the World* speaks directly to this issue. A professor at Boston University, Prothero observes that the claim that all religions are fundamentally the same is an insult to all religions, because they have different benchmarks and different goals and different frameworks and different worldviews.

Indeed, the greater global reality is that all religions are *not* fundamentally the same. On a global scale, religion is one of the most significant forces behind violence and conflict. The happy "let's all learn from each other" spirit is naïve, at least globally speaking.

A weekly bulletin from a group called Compass Direct reports on persecution of Christians in specific and religious persecution in general around the world. The largest countries represented in these reports are Nigeria and India, but China, Egypt, Mexico, Pakistan and Central Asian countries appear regularly. When I serve in Nigeria, almost 100 percent of my colleagues know personally someone who had died in violence between Muslims and Christians in the middle and northern regions of that country. Conflicts about faith are real and deeply rooted in the histories of these countries. For those of us in North America who tend to look forward and disregard the past, understanding these conflicts can be a challenge (see "Utilitarian Historians" at the end of this chapter).

As we prepare ourselves for service in the contemporary world, we need to understand what it means to proclaim the one and only Savior Jesus Christ in a religiously diverse and historically divided world. How can we assert our faith while maintaining civility and a tolerance for plurality? How can we live as what Tim Tennent calls "engaged exclusivists," adhering to the uniqueness of Jesus Christ as Savior while graciously engaging in dialogue with people of other world religions?[9]

Migrated, globalized, urbanized. Finally, ours is a world of migration, globalization and urbanization. A book titled *Word Made Global: Stories of African Christianity in New York City* features a specific case study of African church plants based in New York City from churches out of Liberia, Ghana and Nigeria.[10] The Redeemed Christian Church of God in Nigeria has already planted five hundred churches across North America.

Renewal in churches in Europe is attributed to the migrations of Christians from Africa, Asia and Latin America. If you go to the largest church in Europe, you'll find it pastored by a Nigerian missionary. The largest church in London is pastored by a Nigerian missionary, and one of the five largest churches in New York City is pastored by a Nigerian missionary.

Migrations of people both by immigration and by international study may arguably be the greatest hope for the church of the secularized postmodern world. Philip Jenkins, in his book *God's Continent,* addresses the issue of whether or not Islam will become the dominant religion in Europe. He points out that when people assume that Europe will become exceedingly Muslim, they forget that a large number of immigrants coming into Europe from other African countries are Christians fleeing Islam.[11]

In another of his books, Jenkins discusses the impact of migration into the United States with the summary: "How an already Christian country became even more Christian by immigration."[12] Bill Taylor of the World Evangelical Alliance Mission Commission sees this migration as a part of the continuum of God at work in the world: "Migration of peoples has been key in the advance of the gospel since Pentecost. What can we learn from the tsunami of peoples coming to the United States?"[13]

In terms of migrations, globalization and urbanization, we are now in what *Time* magazine calls the "Chindian Century."[14] Journalist Zoher Abdoolcarim of *Time* asks, which of these two economies will formulate the future of this next century: China or India? Will China's model of business or India's model of democracy? The idea of the "Chindian Century" reminds us that we are seeing not only the migrations of people, but also the migrations of productivity and the migrations of power away from North America.

The bottom line? Power now lies in places where it didn't exist before, and we are the ones called to get used to it.

Questions and Next Steps

1. Which—if any—of the data or statistics in this section surprised you?

2. As you think of your fellowship or local church, how would you answer the question, "Where are we now?" when it comes to understanding and relating to the global church?

UTILITARIAN HISTORIANS

When I studied in seminary back in the 1970s, I took the required church history courses, but I found them boring and disconnected to the great ministry that I envisioned in my future.[1] My studies in mission history started with the Moravians and William Carey, with apparent disregard for the 1,700 years of Christian history that preceded them.

Why? I was a utilitarian historian: if I could find some story in our Christian past that assisted me in proving my point or illustrating my lesson, I cited it. Otherwise, I entered ministry with a distinctively forward-looking, ahistorical approach. We were looking forward to Y2K! There was little time to look back.

As I've aged, I have grown in my desire to know where the Christian movement has come from so that I can better understand where we are going. I realize now that everything we do—including our understanding of the multiple cultures of our world—must be built on a connection to history. Where do we fit in the ongoing historical purposes of God? How would the church from other eras view situations like HIV/AIDS or globalization or a war against terrorism? How does what I'm doing now connect with the work of God throughout history?

As one dedicated to being a practitioner in ministry, I seldom take time for reflective questions like these. A life of ongoing study often gets sacrificed on the altar of urgency. I study, but mostly for the next class, the next task, the next sermon, the next writing project.

Perhaps "staying connected to history" challenges me because I am an American with an ingrained American worldview. We Americans tend to think mostly about the present or the future and very little about our connection to the past. I don't even know my great-grandfather's name. A friend in Lebanon can trace his lineage back to the Phoenicians in 300 B.C.!

In the comic strip *Peanuts*, Lucy is writing a paper on church history. In the first panel, she writes, "To understand church history, we must go back to the very beginning." In the second panel she continues, "Our pastor was born in 1942."

When missionaries report on the "history of missions," we often sound like Lucy: "Our founder first left for overseas missions in 1823." That's the way many of us American Christians think. We don't connect ourselves much to a global religion that originated in the Middle East. We forget that we're part of a historical faith that has included councils and Crusades, popes and problems. (Try telling a conservative evangelical that monks in the Catholic church preserved his Bible, and you'll see what I mean.)

Connecting our ministry to history especially challenges any of us who find ourselves in popular North American culture. Our society tends to disregard history, because we've adapted an experiential view of history in which history does not matter. What matters is *what the history means to me.*

I found getting connected to my Christian history both comforting and challenging. I am comforted to see the sovereign hand of God through the centuries. I am encouraged when I see how God worked through frail, sinful people to accomplish his purposes. I am inspired by those who willingly laid down their lives so that others might experience the love of God through Jesus Christ.

But I am also challenged because by connecting to Christian history, I must accept both the good and the bad of our past. I cannot stand with the great "cloud of witnesses" of Hebrews 11 without accepting the fact that this cloud of witnesses from the Old Testament included murderers, liars and adulterers. The New Testament cloud includes cowards and self-absorbed people who preferred not to cross cultures. And the two thousand years after that includes prideful, racially biased, violent people who brought the gospel and the Crusades or the gospel and colonialism.

Christians of the past always brought the gospel wrapped in the errors of their lives and times. David Bosch sees our church history as intertwining theology, missiology and sociology, the lofty and the mundane. He describes the church as "both a theological and a sociological entity, an inseparable union of the divine and the dusty."[2] The fact that Christians have always been, at least in part, products of their times forced me to ask myself, "What are our blind spots in our contemporary Christianity?"

Three specifics serve as examples of how getting connected to history further challenged me. First, I found myself asking how we can reach out to Muslims today when a misguided early church, blaming the Muslims for the fact that Jesus hadn't returned, launched the Crusades. If we've been violent toward Muslims for over one thousand years, how can we overcome this history by reaching out now?

Secondly, history includes traditions. What do I, with my Baptist background, do with the fact that two of the seven accepted Church Councils (the ones we quote in defense of our historical doctrine of Christ), also endorsed the veneration of icons? How does that connection in history affect my relationship with those of the Orthodox faiths?

And finally, when I'm seeking to challenge folks in Nigeria or Uganda to consider crosscultural missions, can I still use my hero David Livingstone as an example? Can I still refer to him as a role model now that I know his stated mission priorities of opening the interior of Africa so that the European missionaries could bring both "Christianity and commerce"?[3]

Connecting to the past serves not only as an encouragement but also as a deterrent to error. Mission agencies cite "new paradigms" for doing missions; fundraisers cite "breakthroughs." We read about the independent church movement in places like Africa, India and China. These fast-growing, dynamic churches stand as a powerful expression of churches that are "self-theologizing."

But are we in danger of operating in historical isolation? Without a connection to the historical Christian faith, any of us can just drift off into autonomous heresy. How can we keep that from happening?

1

The State of the World

Before we discover the answer to the question "Where do we fit in this globalized world?" we need to get a macro-level view of the world we live in: an overview of what is going on in the world and, more specifically, an overview of some of the challenges and opportunities facing the global church.

It goes without saying that we are living in a world of rapid change. For people in my over-fifty age category, the USSR was a defining force in the world throughout our youth and young adulthood. In our younger years, the war in Vietnam helped define the identity of the United States in the world. Dozens of countries celebrated their independence from colonial powers like Great Britain, France and Portugal. And technological advances included a lunar landing, the advent of the Internet and affordable mobile phones.

For readers under the age of twenty-five, the USSR stands alongside historical realities like the Revolutionary War and the Roman Empire: it existed at one time but has no bearing on our lives. Western identity in the world has moved to being defined by wars in Iraq and Afghanistan. Some postcolonial nations, such as India, have risen to economic power. Others have suffered with internal violence and the effects of religious nationalism. And technology has become the dominant force linking our world through social media, satellite communications and global interconnectivity.

In terms of the changes ahead, Patrick Johnstone identifies nine global challenges.[1] These are: (1) *Population growth*, which is occurring especially in economically challenged areas of the world. (2) *Migration*, including demographic implications of trends like Europe being 17 percent Muslim by the year 2050. (3) *Urbanization*, which means ten cities will exceed thirty million each by 2050, and all the related challenges of urban poverty. (4) *Health and disease*, including issues like HIV/AIDS. (5) *Climate change* and its impact on the poor. (6) *The economy*, especially the staggering gaps between rich and poor. (7) *Energy resources*, especially decreasing supply, increasing demand and increasing pollution. (8) *Politics and freedom*, including human rights violations and local wars. (9) *Water resources*, especially the potential for water wars in places like the Middle East.

Feeling Overwhelmed?
When we look at the speed of change and the needs of our world, we may become timid and uncertain of how to be involved. We are living in a time similar to the great transitions that the people of God faced in the Bible. Remember the account in Numbers 13 of the twelve spies sent out to scope out the challenges of the Promised Land? They went and saw awesome opportunities ahead and a beautiful, fertile land. But they were overwhelmed by the challenges: huge people, fortified cities and insurmountable obstacles. The naysayers' report exaggerated the challenges, describing the city walls as virtually impenetrable and the people as giants. Joshua and Caleb, however, gave the minority report of faith: "Yes, the challenges are great, but by God's power, we can do this" (paraphrase of Num 13:30). The people rebelled against Caleb and Joshua's report, and the result was forty years of wandering in the desert.

This story reminds us that navigating uncharted territory and facing giant challenges requires faith. But it also reminds us that

- faith is not a natural human response: our instinct is to run from challenges.

- fear is an understandable response to the discomforts of change and desire to stay the way we've always been. It's easy to exaggerate the challenges and run the other way. And yes, bad news is contagious!

- the people of faith want to move ahead, which is a good reminder of why reading this book with a small group, in which you can talk through the challenges ahead together, will be helpful.

In the pages that follow, I'll give you my version of a spy report: what I see in terms of mission involvement in a globalized world. I'll identify the giants along the way, but I also hope that, unlike Joshua and Caleb did with the Israelites, I can persuade you to join me and others who, by faith, believe that there is a place for all of us in the global church.

Nine "Greats"

I already stated that it's rather presumptuous to think that I'm going write about the "state of the whole world" in a few short pages. But I want to try to give you an overview for three reasons. My first purpose is informational: I hope that you'll read something here that you did not already know. My second purpose is encouragement: I hope you'll find something here that will leave you thinking, *Wow! It's amazing to learn of what God is doing in the world.* I hope that, as a follower of Jesus, you'll discover afresh that you are part of God's work and of a global Christian community. My third purpose is challenge. In the nine points that follow, I hope that one or two might create in you some sense of where you want to dive in. Some of the topics I cover will require that people dedicate their whole lives to that specific issue. As the church around the world is growing qualitatively and quantitatively, we need people from every walk of life and from all nations who are committed to being involved in making the church into what Jesus wants it to be. Other topics might require fewer external changes to one's life but no less of an internal reorientation to a new way of thinking about missions in a globalized world.

I'll offer nine headings designed to give us a global overview, and I'm going to use the word *great* to describe them all. Building on some of the themes mentioned earlier, these nine categories enlarge our vision for the challenges we face together around the world. I underscore some and introduce others simply to help us realize that as Christians, we are part of a huge world that exceeds seven billion fellow humans.

When we live in North America, we can easily think, "I'm part of the happening place," or, "Our issues *are* the global issues." But it's humbling to remember that the United States and Canada together represent somewhere between 5 and 6 percent of the world's population. What this means is that roughly 94 percent of the world lives outside of our two nations. God is powerfully at work beyond ourselves, and we need to know about it so that we can join his work.

The Great Transition
Sometime in the 1980s, statisticians reported that the worldwide church of Jesus Christ was, for the first time since the first century, predominately non-Western. In other words, most of our Christian brothers and sisters live in the Southern Hemisphere and the Eastern Hemisphere. Even though the Western world has dominated Christianity for much of Christian history, Christianity is now primarily a nonwhite, non-Western, nonwealthy religion.

In his book *The Next Christendom*, Philip Jenkins writes that if you want to imagine a typical Christian in the world, think of a poor woman in a slum in São Paulo, Brazil, or a poor woman in a village in Nigeria.[2] Our Christian brothers and sisters are fundamentally from other places. If current growth continues, Africa will be the most Christian continent on earth by 2025.

This Great Transition also includes the connectivity of our world.

Globalization is connecting the world in a way it has never been before. In that process, more and more churches from more and more countries are owning the vision to be part of the global Christian missionary enterprise. We hear it in the phrase that the church is going "from every nation to every nation."

We attend a church that meets in Lexington, Massachusetts. Lexington, where the Revolutionary War started, is a key location in American history. One Sunday morning, I experienced firsthand something of this Great Transition from American history to Majority World history. After the service, I met a young man by the name of Isaac Oyibo. Immediately I recognized that his is an African name.

"Isaac, where are you from?" I asked.

"I'm from Nigeria," he replied.

"Wonderful!" I said. "Are you one of the many international students in the Boston area?"

"No, sir."

"Are you here with one of the international companies based in Boston, getting some training?" I asked then.

"No, sir," came his reply.

"Then, Isaac, what brings you to Boston?" I asked.

"I am a missionary from my church in Nigeria," Isaac answered. "We have sent missionaries to Boston because we heard you need the gospel here. We have seen your movies; we know that your country needs missionaries."

It's a Great Transition.

Another example. I first attended the Urbana Missions Conference in 1973, when more than ten thousand Christian students from North America came together to hear the challenge toward global, crosscultural missions. Since that first Urbana experience, I have had the privilege of attending a conference in Nairobi, where 1,500 students from Tanzania, Uganda and Kenya gathered to contemplate God's call into missions. I have attended similar conferences focused on student mobilization for global mission in Sri Lanka, Indonesia,

Taiwan, Ghana, Cuba and Nigeria. At all of these events, thousands of young people were zealously evaluating where God wants them in the world. They represent the future of this Great Transition.

The global church now owns the message as never before. We're all part of that commandment from Jesus to go and preach the gospel to Jerusalem, Judea, Samaria and to the ends of the earth (Acts 1:8). As a colleague from Fiji reminded me, "*Your* Jerusalem is *my* ends of the earth." In other words, the "ends of the earth" mandate varies depending on your starting point. The global church is seeing its responsibility to spread the gospel from every nation to every nation.

Mark Noll illustrates the global shift of Christianity from the historic centers of Christendom to the Majority World. In *The New Shape of World Christianity*, he observes: "This past Sunday it's possible that more Christian believers attended church in China than in all of so-called Christian Europe. Yet in 1970 there were no legally functioning churches in all of China and only in 1971 did the Chinese government allow for one Protestant and one Catholic Church. But now, some people estimate there might be a hundred million Christians in China." Noll continues: "This past Sunday more Anglicans attended the church in each of the countries of Kenya, South Africa, Tanzania and Uganda than Anglicans attended church in Britain, Canada and all of the Episcopalian churches in the United States combined. And Nigeria had four times as many Anglicans as those other countries." He adds that there were more Presbyterians worshiping in Ghana than in Scotland, where Presbyterianism has its roots, and that there were more members attending Pentecostal Assemblies of God churches in Brazil than those attending churches of the two largest Pentecostal denominations in the United States.

And perhaps most representative of the Great Transition, Noll states, "This past week in Great Britain at least 15,000 Christian foreign missionaries were hard at work evangelizing the locals. Most of these missionaries are from Africa and Asia."[3]

In this regard, Bill Dyrness of Fuller Theological Seminary observes, "Missions is now mutual exchange among multiple centers of influence and learning and resources traveling all directions, not only from here to there."[4]

I experienced this firsthand on a layover in Germany on my way to a conference in St. Petersburg, Russia. To combat jet lag, I walked around town in the early evening, just trying to stay awake. As I walked, I saw people by the dozens relaxing after work, sitting at open-air cafes and enjoying their meals.

In the distance, I began hearing the cadences of a street preacher. So here is the scene: scores of Germans workers—historical descendants of Martin Luther, founder of the Protestant Reformation—were sitting in the square, drinking their steins of beer and eating their snacks. Meanwhile, a young Christian evangelist was standing in the crowd, preaching his heart out, while his colleagues handed out Christian literature.

The preacher was from Angola. His coworkers were from Kenya and Malaysia. That's a picture of the Great Transition: from every nation to every nation.

As we from North America confront this Great Transition, we can celebrate the amazing growth of the gospel. But it may also cause us to start wrestling with where we fit in the world. It will challenge our commitment to servanthood: are we needed anymore? Is there a role for us? If the Majority World churches are autonomous, does that mean that we are now left out?[5] Are we in the West in danger of being marginalized by the initiative of the church in the Majority World? Will we become globally irrelevant? Or have we already become so?

The Great Migration

I referred earlier to the vast movement of peoples in our world, but this great sociological phenomena needs expansion. The Great Migration, as I use it here, has to do with the vast movement of peoples from nation to nation.[6] It happens for reasons related to economics, politics and personal freedoms. It occurs legally and illegally, with documented and undocumented peoples. And it is occurring in many places beyond just the United States and Canada. It is transforming Europe and creating major subcultures in Africa, Latin America, Asia, and the Middle East.

When you arrive at the international airport in Manila, the Philippines, there are three lines for passport control: one for visitors, one for citizens/residents and one for OFW: Overseas Filipino Workers. More than 10 percent of the citizens of the Philippines are working in some other country of the world. When we visited the Cayman Islands in the Caribbean, every person checking us out at the supermarket was from the Philippines. Hotel workers in Europe, airport workers in the United Arab Emirates and nurses in the United States and Canada: many are Filipinos.

Todd Johnson, global statistics expert and coauthor of the *Atlas of World Christianity*, writes, "Migration is increasing religious and ethnic diversity around the world. Two hundred million people are on the move today, carrying with them their cultural and religious backgrounds. At least 720 million have now settled permanently outside of their culture's main country. Almost half of these are Christians, representing about 16 percent of all Christians. There are also Muslims, Hindus and Buddhists living in large numbers outside of their homelands."[7]

With these mass migrations of peoples, we may have the opportunity to reach people who were, up to this point, considered unreached—not because we went to *their* place but because they came to *our* place. The world is changing before our eyes. In Toronto, one of the most international cities in North America, a pastor observed, "God called us to go to all nations. We didn't go, so he's bringing all nations to us!"

While traveling in Phoenix, Arizona, I began a conversation with my taxi driver, Abdul. I discovered that he is a Sudanese Muslim from northern Sudan. I have no idea if he's ever heard the gospel, but I cannot speak Arabic. Most likely I could never talk to him about Jesus if I went to his hometown in Sudan. But he speaks English now, and he's in my world. Jesus' command in Matthew 28:19 to "go and make disciples of all nations" now includes praying for and sharing my faith with Abdul. This Great Migration affects the whole world, not just the United States. While visiting with a friend in Cairo, Egypt, we discussed his future. He is an Egyptian citizen but he served many years as an English teacher in Libya. His opportunities in Libya had ended, although he loves the people of Libya. He was wondering, "What does God have for me now?"

We talked about the possibility that God was calling him not to Libya but to Libyans. I asked him, "Do I remember that you speak Spanish?"

"Yes," he replied.

"Havana, Cuba, could be God's next call for you," I said. "Years ago, Muammar Gaddafi and Fidel Castro had a friendship. Now there are hundreds of Libyan students in Havana reachable for the gospel."

In our own greater Boston region, we have found out that there are more than twelve thousand Moroccan Muslims in two nearby towns. I met a woman who had come to the United States in 2000 through a ministry called World Relief. She was resettled as a refugee from Somalia. Over the next decade she became a follower of Jesus, and now she's looking for an opportunity to find other Somalis so that she can share her relationship with Jesus with them.

That's what God is doing through these mass migrations of people: from every nation, to every nation, back to every nation. And the Great Migration of peoples is providing new opportunities: first to reach out to those who have never heard the gospel, and second to join with Christian immigrants as they help us reach our own nation.

Several years ago I started praying for the isolated, difficult-to-reach nation of Bhutan, a country in the Himalayas locked in a Tibetan-style of Buddhism. When my wife, Christie, and I visited a young couple serving as dorm parents at nearby Wellesley College, we had no idea that it would connect us to Bhutan.

Before we joined our friends for dinner, they said, "We know that you have been praying for Bhutan for years. We want you to meet our only Bhutanese student." So they took us over and introduced us to a young woman from Bhutan, a sophomore at the time. We had a brief conversation, and I expressed my interest in Bhutan. Then we joined our friends for dinner. "Do you know the young woman you just met? Did you recognize her name?" they asked me.

If I had prayed more intelligently for the leaders of Bhutan, I might have recognized the name, but I didn't. "The young woman you just met is the favorite daughter of the favorite wife of the king of Bhutan," our friends told us. "You just met the princess of Bhutan."

A future leader of an almost impossible-to-reach country was studying ten miles from my home. God is moving the world to hear the gospel through the Great Migration.

While visiting a church in the eastern United States, I experienced this move of God again. As an outreach to international students in their area, the church sponsored a welcome dinner every September. (I was the "Welcome to America" banquet speaker.) The free food and the church's reputation for international hospitality attracted many students. In addition to their local outreach, this church had a global vision as well, expressed in part by adopting and praying for an unreached people group.[8] The church had adopted a people group from South China called the Miao people. All over the church there were posters inviting people to "Pray for the Miao." The posters had statistics about the people group, population information, how many known Christians there are in the area, where the Miao are located and which missionaries are working with these people. Every member of the church was committed to pray for the Miao people.

As I was standing outside the banquet hall, a young man approached me. I guessed that he was from China. He said, "Excuse me, sir, are you from this church?"

"No, I'm not from this church," I said. "This is my first time here."

"Me too," he replied. "This is my first time in any church. I am from the People's Republic of China; I am a master's degree student. I am just starting the semester, but I heard there was food, so I came."

I welcomed him to the United States and to the church, and he continued, "I need to ask another question. What is this sign?" He pointed to one of the signs that read, "Pray for the Miao." I tried my best to explain this prayer strategy to a student who was unchurched and had no idea of religious jargon. "Well, these people are followers of Jesus and they're trying to help other people know about the love of Jesus," I began. "So they've invited their church to pray for this ethnic minority group from south China."

"It is amazing!" he said.

"What is amazing?" I replied, a little confused.

"I am Miao!" he said earnestly. "These are my people."

"Well, this church has been praying for you," I answered. I introduced him to church leaders as the young man they had been praying for. God is at work.

When the peoples of the world migrate into our neighborhoods, it's an invitation from God. Some might serve them by helping them get their documentation in order. Others might start an English as a Second Language program. Others can simply provide hospitality.

The Great Migration also has implications for our efforts at reaching our own cultures. Many of the people coming from other countries to North America are already Christians, and these newcomers often come with a great zeal to preach the gospel. A leader in a church in Illinois told me that their church's commitment to evangelism was resurrected when a Ugandan family joined the church. "They put us to shame with their boldness in proclaiming Jesus," he said. "God used their example to awaken in us a greater burden for the nonbelieving people in our own communities."

The Great Divides

The third challenge facing the world relates to divisions between people. Consider two significant Great Divides in the church.

The economic divide. The most conspicuous divide is between the rich and the poor. If most of the Christian church now is in the Majority World, most of our Christian brothers and sisters are economically less advantaged than we are. What does that mean for us? How can we use our generosity without creating unhealthy economic dependency? Globalization is not necessarily solving the problem of the rich-poor divide. While some might be moving into the middle class by working in call centers in India, many others are still suffering.

My reference to call centers is an allusion to the work of author Thomas Friedman. If you have read Friedman, you may know that he tends to exaggerate the benefits of globalization.[9] But India is much more than one big, shiny call center. In reality, even if three hundred million Indians are working in middle-class jobs, that could leave some seven hundred million Indians who are still suffering in poverty, many in crippling poverty. India is just that vast.

The rich-poor divide calls us to think about things like caring for the poor and standing for justice-related issues. It calls us to wrestle with issues like microfinance and business as mission. It calls us to wrestle with 1 John 3:16-18: "This is how we know what love is: Jesus Christ laid down his life for us. And we ought to lay down our lives for our brothers and sisters. If anyone has material possessions and sees a brother or sister in need but has no pity on them, how can the love of God be in that person? Dear children, let us not love with words or speech but with actions and in truth."

Because we in North America often have the world's goods and we now see our brothers and sisters in need, how will we respond? Consider a story told by Zac Niringiye, the assistant bishop of the Anglican diocese in Kampala, Uganda. He described how Uganda had started to reverse the trend of increasing numbers of HIV/AIDS cases to the point that new cases of and deaths from HIV/AIDS were actually on the decline. "The secret was when the church owned the problem for ourselves," Zac says. "When we said, 'People have AIDS,' or 'Sinners have AIDS,' we stayed aloof and judgmental. But when we begin to realize that HIV/AIDS was affecting many of the Christian families in our churches, we changed our language. We

started to say, 'My family has AIDS.' That's when we got involved."[10]
This story forces us to ask ourselves this question: what struggles
is my global family facing? Members of my family in many of the
great urban centers of the world suffer from economic deprivation.
What challenges does my family face in places like Sri Lanka or India
or Egypt or Bolivia?

The theological divide. How dependent on God are we in North
America? Our non-Western brothers and sisters often put us to
shame. In North America, many Christians relegate miracles, signs
and wonders to the first century. Our worldviews are so influenced
by the Enlightenment that we really don't comprehend the miracle-
driven, spirit-aware world of the Bible.

In practical terms, many of us in the North American church are
what used to be called *cessationists:* people who believe that the gifts
of miracles, signs and wonders were only for the first century.
Healing, raising the dead, visions, signs, wonders and miracles:
many of us believe that these were primarily for the age of the
apostles and the book of Acts, not for now.

My advice: if you want to be a cessationist, don't travel! The church
in the Majority World did not get the memo. When somebody gets
sick, the first thing they do is pray and anoint them with oil. If
somebody falls out of a third-floor window, they don't dial 911; they
ask, "What did the Christians do in Acts?"

On my first visit to Nigeria, a young man was assigned to carry my
briefcase. We got to talking one day and I said to him, "Robert, how
did you become a Christian?" He replied, "Oh, Brother John over
there raised me from the dead."

After recovering from my surprise, I asked him, "Why do my Nigerian friends see more miracles than we do in the United States?"

"You have more doctors," he replied matter-of-factly. "If God doesn't
heal us, we die. You just have more doctors." Using good theology, he
concluded, "God heals you one way, and he heals us another."

The church that is dependent upon Jesus sees God's power in a way that the church that is dependent on itself does not. We in North America have a lot to learn about being more dependent on God from churches in Africa, Asia and Latin America.

Illustrating this theological divide, Mark Noll summarizes the theological questions being asked in the Majority World church.[11] He writes about the questions that the global church is asking that we in the Western church don't usually ask:

"How close is the world of spirits to everyday life?" In other words, what role do my deceased ancestors play in my world? How does the Holy Spirit's power manifest itself?

"What is the unit of salvation?" In other words, rather than the highly individualistic view of salvation promoted by Western theology, can a person be saved as a representative of their family? The phrase "you and all your household will be saved," which appears in Acts 11:14 (and a similar phrase again in Acts 16:31), means something different to Christians who come from more communal societies.

This theological divide is by no means uncrossable, but it calls us to listen more and to dialogue with our non-Western brothers and sisters so that we gain a better understanding of global theology.[12]

The Great Wall

My fourth and fifth challenges use visual images to represent something bigger. When I refer to the Great Wall, I'm obviously alluding to the amazing structure that strings across China. As such, it represents the twenty-first-century challenge of China itself. Already an economic superpower, the People's Republic of China will be a shaping force across the world. Religiously, China represents not only one of the fastest growing churches in the world, but also the country with the highest number of unreached peoples. Economically, politically, religiously and perhaps militarily, China is in all of our futures.

(Let me pause here to address readers of Chinese heritage. If you have a Chinese heritage, I want to exhort you to look at that like the apostle Paul looked at his Roman citizenship [see Acts 22:25-29]. If you speak Mandarin or have dual citizenship, you face opportunities in this most populous of nations. There are openings in a country that was hidden from the world from 1949 until the 1970s. In 1973, there was not one chance for any Westerner to go to China. Now all of a sudden, doors have been flung open for English teachers, businesspeople and more.)

The Great Wall of China is immense and impressive. It represents a huge desire of people to separate themselves from each other. There are long stretches of the wall that go no particular place and then just end. The wall was constructed to keep people out. Much of the wall goes up and down difficult-to-navigate mountains. When you stand on top of the wall, you wonder, "If my enemy could ascend the steep mountain on which the wall sits, what's the extra twelve feet?"

As a symbol, the Great Wall represents not only the challenge of China; it also represents the great divide between peoples who have heard the gospel and those who have not: the unreached peoples of the world. There are still an estimated two billion people (almost one-third of the world) who have never received an invitation to respond to the love of God as demonstrated by the death and resurrection of Jesus Christ.

These are not people who have rejected Jesus; these are those who have never heard who Jesus Christ is. The wall between the gospel "haves" and the gospel "have-nots" needs to be scaled if these people are to be invited to God's global family.

Reflecting on this wall, Todd Johnson observes:

Christians are out of contact with Muslims, Hindus and Buddhists. Recent research reveals that as many as 86 percent of all Muslims, Hindus and Buddhists do not personally know a Christian. This must be viewed negatively in light of the strong biblical theme of incarnation, which is at the heart of Christian witness. Christians should know and love their neighbors! In the twenty-first century, it is important to realize that the responsibility for reaching Muslims, Hindus and Buddhists is too large for the missionary enterprise. While missionaries will always be at the forefront of innovative strategies, the whole church needs to participate in inviting people of other faiths to consider Jesus Christ.[13]

In addition to the wall between the gospel "haves" and gospel "have-nots," there are other symbolic walls, especially ethnic divides between peoples, both in our own country and around the world. Racism, ethnocentrism and interethnic conflict call us as Christians to the ministries of peacemaking and reconciliation.

In Southern Sudan, shortly after the new nation was formed, historical ethnic conflicts arose, resulting in attempted genocides as the Murle people and the Nuer exchanged retaliatory strikes in an effort to wipe each other out.[14] In Myanmar, where there have been glimmers of hope that the military dictatorship might move toward greater democracy, ethnic warfare between the Kachin minority group and the Burmese majority have observers wondering if reforms are possible.[15]

These interethnic clashes affect the global church as well. In North America, the Sunday morning worship hour is still regarded as the most racially segregated hour in the week. In Kenya, one of the most Christian countries of Africa, the Kenyan church was humbled in 2007. After disputed presidential elections between the candidates, who came from Kikuyu and Luo ethnic groups, interethnic violence broke out, killing hundreds and displacing thousands. And the violence included clashes between Christians. Church leaders realized that the great ethnic walls that they thought had collapsed were still in place.

Nowhere is this Great Wall more evident than in the barriers that exist between world religions. The advance of world religions, like the migrations of people, is going on all over the world. Although most migrating peoples are peace-loving people in search of a better lifestyle, the radical fringe element and religious extremism are creating one of the greatest challenges for our brothers and sisters around the world in places like China, Indonesia, India, the Middle East and many other locales.[16]

It's important to note that these barriers and religious extremism are not exclusively from the other world religions. Violence in northern and central Nigeria has included both Muslims burning churches and Christians burning mosques. People who call themselves Christians in places like France and Switzerland, or a Qur'an-burning pastor in Florida, have provoked hostility and resentment by their harsh and disrespectful treatment of people from other religions. All of this is part of what I'm calling the Great Wall between religiously diverse peoples.

Miriam Adeney notes a similar wall in Iran. "Some estimate as many as 800,000 followers of Jesus are inside Iran," Adeney writes. "But following Jesus in Iran is costly. Some get fired, other imprisoned, even killed. Muslim regimes do not foster religious freedom. Conversion out of Islam is prohibited. Resistance to conversion is increasing."[17]

The walls of separation between peoples are immense, and they challenge the global church. We need Christians who are peacemakers, reconcilers and bridge-builders between people in conflict.

The Great Barrier Reef

The fifth great challenge is also symbolic. Like the Great Wall of China, the Great Barrier Reef is supposedly visible from the moon. It's the largest living structure in the world, stretching for hundreds of miles under water off the eastern coast of Australia. I refer to the Great Barrier Reef here as a representation of the great global issue of the environment.

Whether human-caused or a result of natural cycles (or both), climate change is a serious matter, and Christians need to be involved in creation care. When the environment gets destroyed, the poorest people suffer worst. When a tsunami hit Sri Lanka in 2004, the people who suffered the most were the poorest people.[18] So the environment is not just an environmental issue; it's a rich-poor issue. A publication from the National Association of Evangelicals identifies this connection between environmental degradation and poverty: "Changes in the environment interact with poverty to worsen its effects by increasing conflicts and migration while decreasing the ability of the poor to improve their well-being."[19] When the land becomes barren, rich people can move to another home. In contrast, poor people lose their farms, become destitute and move to a refugee camp. *Sun Come Up* was the first documentary to introduce me to the term *environmental refugees*. It describes the south Pacific Islander people known as the Cartaret and their plight of losing everything as the rising waters of the Pacific swallowed their homeland.

Put simply, the global mission of God calls some people to go out as dedicated church planters to unreached people groups. But it calls some to serve as dedicated tree planters in eroded areas, some to work toward providing clean water for those who do not have access and others to address the problems of hazardous waste. All these activities are part of God's kingdom work in redeeming people and the world.

The Great Commission

Challenges number six and seven are biblical "greats." Our sixth is summarized in what we know as the Great Commission, or Jesus' last words in Matthew 28:18-20: "All authority in heaven and on earth has been given to me. Therefore go and make disciples of all nations, baptizing them . . . and teaching them to obey everything I have commanded you. And surely I am with you always, to the very end of the age."[20]

The reason that I bring up the Great Commission as a global issue facing the church around the world is the call to "make disciples." In the last century, the global church has excelled in making converts and fostering decisions. Evangelistic sermons, literature and films have introduced millions to the gospel story. Many have made an initial response.

We have not done a great job in making disciples, however, either in North America or in the Majority World. Do you understand the difference? The person who raises his or her hand at the end of a presentation might be a convert but not a disciple. Jesus didn't say go into the world and make *converts*; he said go into all the world and make *disciples*.

Becoming a disciple and making disciples is tough work. It means digging deep into our lives, which will show us a lot of things needing to be remade by the strength of the Holy Spirit. Becoming and making disciples takes time. Making converts can happen pretty fast; making disciples can take a lifetime. Through this Great Commission, Jesus reminds us that the issue is not to make the church broader but deeper.

In the United States and around the world, leaders sometimes say, "Our greatest problem here [in this country] is that the church is miles wide and inches deep." Obedience to the Great Commission suffers because nominal Christians, who have been momentarily "converted," do not grow in integrity or character or biblical knowledge or Christian living. These superficial decisions are not necessarily integrated into the way they live, treat their spouses, operate in their community or participate in business and politics. We need disciples.

When we think about the Great Commission and our part in it, there are four things to remember.

All authority. Jesus stands up in front of the disciples and says, "All authority in heaven and on earth has been given to me." This is a post-resurrection appearance of Jesus, so when Jesus said this, if he extended his hands, the light was shining through the holes in his hands. In other words, he is saying: "Disciples, I've just conquered death; all authority is mine. You don't need to go into the world afraid about proclaiming absolute truth. I've conquered death to tell you I am that Truth. You don't have to be afraid of how you're going to get treated; all authority belongs to me. Nothing is going to happen to you that I'm not going to allow."

We go out into the world in his authority.

All nations. If you have taken a mission course, you know that Jesus' phrase "all nations" means not just all the geopolitical nations recognized on maps. Jesus is referring to all the ethnic-specific units (*ethne* = "nations"). So Jesus is not just telling us to go to China, but to the Han people and the Miao people and the Uygur people and all the other diverse ethnic groups. We are to go to all the ethnicities of the world. If we're looking for opportunities to evangelize, we need to be thinking not just about nations but about the specific people from those nations.

All things. Third, Jesus says, "Teaching them to obey *everything* I have commanded you." Not just the happy things. Not just the user-friendly, seeker-friendly, I-feel-fulfilled-with-Jesus things. But things like taking up the cross daily, laying down our lives, putting other people first. In other words, we are to teach—and obey—even the uncomfortable things.

And the goal is not just teaching everything; the dissemination of Christian truths and theologies is not the end goal. The end goal is *obedience.*

Always. Jesus concludes with an awesome promise to those who want to shape their lives by the Great Commission: "I am with you *always.*" Wherever you are going, Jesus is there with you.

In summary, the Great Commission challenge comes in the form of four superlatives. Jesus says that he has *all authority* to send us to *all the world's ethnic groups* to teach them to obey *all the things* that he commanded and that he will be with us *always.*

How many of us grow fearful when we think about what God might call us to in this world of global Christianity? What if he calls me to stay single? Or to go to challenging places like the Middle East or some megacity or a remote village in Nepal? Or to sacrifice financially?

In response to fear, remember the most common command in the Bible: *don't be afraid.* A Nigerian brother told me that this command— Don't be afraid / fear not / don't be anxious—appears 365 times in the Bible, once for every day of the year. "Don't fear" doesn't mean that we'll never be afraid. It simply means that we don't have to be ruled by our fears. Psalm 56:3 says, "When I am afraid, I put my trust in you." We do get afraid. We arrive somewhere on a short-term or long-term crosscultural mission trip and we say to ourselves, "What have I done?" or "Why am I here?" or "What was I thinking?" Many times I have had to wait at an airport for a long time for someone to come and pick me up. I sometimes pray, "Jesus, I'm giving you to 7:30 and then I'm really going to freak out." And more than a few times, someone shows up at 7:29. People sometimes ask me, "Have you ever been afraid?" Yeah! In some situations, I would be stupid *not* to be afraid. But Jesus goes with us everywhere. Jesus doesn't dwell exclusively in North America. As we face the challenges already mentioned and the issues that future chapters will raise, it's easy to want to shrink away in fear. The Great Commission is a reminder that we go into this world under the authority of the risen Christ and with the assurance of his presence.

The Great Compassion

Challenge number seven actually precedes the Great Commission in the Bible. Peter Kuzmič from Gordon-Conwell Theological Seminary often says it this way: "We need to preach out of Matthew, not just the Great Commission out of Matthew 28 but *the Great Compassion* out of Matthew 25."

Kuzmič's point is this: when Jesus says "teaching them to obey everything," he is including his teaching from Matthew 25. In the story of the judgment of all nations (Mt 25:31-46), Jesus tells us that the way we treat the poor, the marginalized, the hungry, the naked, the prisoner and the homeless is the way that we treat him.

How we treat the people needing compassion and justice and care and advocacy is the criteria of his judgment. They are fully part of our mission in the world. One of the challenges of the church around the world is not just to proclaim the resurrected Jesus of the Great Commission, but to proclaim the compassion of Jesus by our deeds.

There is no room for a one-sided gospel. We preach Jesus by our words and by our deeds. We preach Jesus by teaching English or by helping people understand how to manage food stamps. We plant churches and we plant trees. We preach Jesus in all areas of life.

How do we as Christians be more intentional with respect to compassion? I look for any way I can to connect my life to God's world. A few years ago, it dawned on me that I could enlarge my global praying by praying for the country on the label of my clothes. In other words, the world is in my closet.

I have a friend in Sri Lanka who is on the staff of the International Fellowship of Evangelical Students. He is a wonderful and brilliant man, and he is fond of telling me what is wrong with the United States. When I go to visit him, I have to fasten my seatbelt and just listen.

On one visit to Sri Lanka, I told him my idea of praying for the country on the label of my clothes. I told him that I sometimes share this idea with my college students. Given that I've been to sweatshops in Sri Lanka where clothes for the Western world are made by poorly paid and sometimes abused workers, I expected him to criticize my idea as one that forgets the plight of the poor. Based on past conversations, I expected that he would equate my "pray for the country on the label of your clothes" suggestion as just another example of American superficiality.

Nevertheless, I gathered my courage and asked, "When I speak to Western audiences, should I encourage people to boycott those stores where sweatshop clothes are made?" I expected to get a full-octave blast against Americanization, globalization and our materialistic corruption of the world. He surprised me with his answer, however, which he spoke in a very sober voice. "No. If your people boycott those clothes, poor people will get poorer. The factory might close, and people getting pennies in a sweatshop will now have to resort to doing something else, maybe worse, like prostitution, in order to feed their families."

"So what shall I tell my listeners?" I asked him. He replied, "Tell people, especially your businesspeople, to become executives for Nike and other multinational corporations that run these factories. In positions of leadership, they can bring a Christian influence of compassion and justice and mercy into that environment. They can make rules of how the factory workers are treated. That could turn a whole village toward the gospel."

Months later, I shared his response with a church in New York City. One fellow approached me and said, "That's a great idea. I'm the representative buyer with a factory we have in Madagascar. I buy jeans from that factory. I sell them on Fifth Avenue; we buy jeans for a dollar and sell them for four hundred dollars. Maybe we can do something."

He contacted the factory liaison in Madagascar and asked how much it would cost if the factory started paying for the school fees for the workers' children, better housing, health care, improved sanitation and more reasonable hours. The buyer was pursuing compassion for these workers.

The buyer got a message back from the liaison representing the factory management. He said that they were very sorry, but such added benefits would quadruple the price for the jeans to four dollars a pair. The buyer decided to authorize it anyway, thus making the "sacrifice" to go from a $399 profit margin down to a $396 profit on the jeans. A Christian used his position of power to bring about compassion and justice for the poor. He was leveraging his position for the poor.

Compassion takes on different shapes. Some might choose to live in an intentional community committed to incarnational ministry with the urban poor. Others might become legal aides who can influence a senator or a member of parliament to make a decision that can empower many poor people. Who knows? We need eyes of compassion toward our world; it is one of the biggest challenges facing the church.

The Great Salvation

Challenges eight and nine are fundamentally personal worldview issues. They relate to the spiritual lenses through which we see the world and our role in it. Number eight I call the Great Salvation. The phrase is crucial, as it applies to many of us who live in places where the Christian church is more than two or three generations old. I take the phrase from Hebrews 2:3: "How shall we escape if we ignore so great a salvation?"

The recipients of the letter to the Hebrews were tired of the opposition and hardships of following Christ. They were in danger of quitting the faith or at least marginalizing it in their lives. The writer of the letter exhorts them to remember the greatness of salvation: the overwhelming reality that God himself came down in the person of Jesus to be the sacrifice for our sins.

You and I might not be contemplating quitting the faith. But we may be marginalizing it in our lives, allowing the allure of a Western lifestyle to dull the edges of our faith. Add to this the challenges of navigating our faith in the midst of a globalized world, and it is easy to understand why we may want to retreat.

Without an invigorated understanding of salvation, Christianity can quickly become nominal, cultural or institutional. My challenge to myself and others is to remember the greatness of salvation that is in Jesus Christ. Don't lose the wonder of what Jesus has done for us. Our Western, affluent lifestyle is incredibly enticing—so much so that it's often easier to desire this lifestyle than it is to desire a lifestyle more compatible with following Jesus.

One of the most famous missionaries of the nineteenth century, C. T. Studd, stated, "If Jesus Christ is God and he died for me, no sacrifice I make is too great." If I say I want to follow Jesus, then I'm saying, "Jesus, in light of everything you've done for me, here I am."

My exhortation is that we don't neglect the gift of salvation. Everything we do in the world is in response to the fact that Jesus picked us up, became flesh for us and then laid down his life for us.

Understanding this Great Salvation is essential, because following Jesus to the ends of the earth is risky. Some followers will have a premature entry into heaven because of where they went. We may not live out the normal American dream. We might not retire to Arizona and play golf or be the shuffleboard champion at our retirement home. We won't live out that dream because we went where Jesus took us. If we understand the awesomeness of salvation, we'll say, "Jesus is so worth it; all other dreams pale by comparison."

A brief tangent for a moment: people sometimes say to Christie and me as we travel to dangerous places, "Remember, Paul, the safest place to be is in the center of God's will." I know that they mean well, but I disagree. The *right* place to be is in the center of God's will, but it might not be the safest place. After all, who is the ultimate person who lived at the center of God's will? Jesus. And his life was far from safe, with false arrest, torture and ultimately a gruesome death on the cross. God may evangelize the people we are called to reach by our martyrdom.

On a journey to Ghana, my host took me to the missionary cemetery where vast numbers of twenty-five- and twenty-six-year-olds were buried. They had died within two years of coming to Ghana or West Africa to bring the gospel. Tradition says that the British missionaries journeyed to West Africa with their earthly goods packed in their own caskets. They knew when they brought the gospel they would not return home. They went to die there. And they did. They didn't last long, but they planted the seed of the gospel. On that same trip, I visited a Pentecostal church in Ghana that is sending missionaries to eighty-five different countries in the world. This can happen now because people came a century ago and laid down their lives.

When we start thinking about the Great Salvation, we realize that we are identified with Jesus, who laid down his life so that we might benefit. "Unless a kernel of wheat falls to the ground and dies . . ." (Jn 12:24).

For many of us, following Jesus in this world will not require literally dying. But it might require downsizing our lifestyle. It might mean taking vacation time to go on a short-term mission trip when we could be just relaxing. In any case, it's all about identifying with Jesus and saying, in light of the Great Salvation, "Jesus, I want to go where you're going and where you want to bring me."

The Great Celebration

If a reminder of the greatness of salvation motivates us to go wherever God leads us, a vision of the Great Celebration will help us stay faithful. This globalized world is not simply about challenges; it is about celebrating. Paul celebrates with the Colossian believers when he writes, "The gospel is bearing fruit and growing throughout the whole world" (Col 1:6).

Earlier I mentioned that I started praying for Bhutan and later met the princess of the country, who at the time was an international student. Two years after that, I had the privilege of teaching a course in Guahati, in the northeastern Indian state of Assam. When I mentioned Bhutan, my prayers and my burden for this country, students laughed and introduced me to their classmate Nima. Nima, my student, was the first Bhutanese Christian I had ever met, more than two decades after starting my Bhutan-focused prayer.

Meeting Nima reminded me of the biblical descriptions of the ultimate Great Celebration. The apostle John sees crowds of worshipers, and these worshipers "sang a new song, saying: 'You are worthy to take the scroll and to open its seals, because you were slain, and with your blood you purchased for God persons from every tribe and language and people and nation'" (Rev 5:9). And again: "After this I looked, and there before me was a great multitude that no one could count, from every nation, tribe, people and language, standing before the throne and before the Lamb. They were wearing white robes and were holding palm branches in their hands. And they cried out in a loud voice: 'Salvation belongs to our God, who sits on the throne, and to the Lamb'" (Rev 7:9-10).

There's going to be a Great Celebration someday, at which people from every tribe and tongue and nation will worship Jesus. Bhutanese Christians like Nima will be there. I pray that the princess will be there. Maybe the Bangladeshi guy who made my sport shirt will be there because I prayed for the country on the label of my clothes. Maybe on the day I prayed, he heard a Christian radio program, which led to a correspondence course, which led to meeting Christians, which after years of friendship led to him becoming a follower of Jesus. Maybe I'll meet him at the Great Celebration. Wouldn't that be awesome? Imagine it! A long-robed, bearded fellow comes over and says, "Hello. My name is Abdul Abdullah from Dhaka, Bangladesh. Thank you for praying for me. I made your shirt."

God works that way. We are part of something bigger. When we go out into the world, we might suffer and incur hardship, but we are participating in God's ultimate party. A Great Celebration day is coming when an uncountable group, speaking thousands of languages from tens of thousands of ethnic backgrounds, will gather to sing praise to the Lamb of God, Jesus, because we're all redeemed by his precious blood.

Read Revelation 5:9 and 7:9 for a vision that will keep you going. When you're struggling to reach out to a Muslim neighbor or to the Buddhist guy in a Thai restaurant, remember that a day is coming when people from every tribe and tongue and nation are going to worship Jesus. And we have the privilege of enlarging that worship service through our lives, our compassion and our testimony to others.

So Where Are We in the World?

In review: we're living in a Great Transition in which Christianity has moved from the Northern Hemisphere to the South, the West to the East.

We're witnessing a Great Migration of peoples for all sorts of reasons, ranging from political to economic to religious. These newcomers will present us with opportunities for compassionate outreach as well as partnership in reaching our own culture.

The world we live in includes two Great Divides. Economically, the rich-poor divide calls us to lives of generosity. Theologically, the ways that we understand God and faith calls us to a globally expanded view of God.

Great Walls, symbolizing the separation of people from each other and from the gospel, call us to be peacemakers and bridge-builders.

The Great Barrier Reef, symbolic of the environmental challenges in our world, calls us to a greater stewardship of the physical world.

The Great Commission exhorts us to be disciples and to make disciples.

The Great Compassion is our mandate to demonstrate the gospel and not just preach it.

With eyes on our Great Salvation through Jesus, we find our motivation for action and sacrifice as we remember what Jesus has done for us.

And the vision of the Great Celebration turns our eyes to the day when people from every tribe, tongue and nation will worship Jesus.

Questions and Next Steps

1. Which of the "greats" (if any) surprised you?

2. Which of the "greats" would you like to discuss or contest with the author?

3. Which of these "greats" might be something you could dedicate yourself to addressing, either locally or globally? How?

4. Given the Great Migration and the Great Wall between peoples, could you consider taking a course to understand other world religions?

A BOOK, A MOVIE, A SONG
Thoughts on the Next Christendom

After a slow reread of *The Next Christendom: The Coming of Global Christianity* by Philip Jenkins, I was stirred again in my thinking about the future of Christian mission, especially for the Western church in which I live and serve.[1] The future Western church will be increasingly the recipient of new missionaries from the South, and, in keeping with the global nature of God's mission, it will continue to send missionaries.

As I read Jenkins, my missiological thinking started blending with my first crosscultural ministry assignment: being a youth worker. Every youth worker knows how to examine the youth culture for symbols, media and music that will provide a truth or a bridge to the gospel. If we can use a rock star or a sports figure, like Paul used statues in Acts 17, we'll do it. Bringing together these two worlds of missiology and youth work, I have summarized the challenges I've gleaned from Jenkins with a book title, a movie title, and a song title.

A book: *Left Behind.* As Jenkins (Philip, not Jerry) aptly points out, the great question facing the Western church is whether it will survive or keep up with the church from the South. Will we in the West simply be "left behind": not in the eschatological sense but ecclesiologically and missiologically? Jenkins, quoting Philip Yancey, reminds us, "God goes where he's wanted."[2] What will that mean in our Western world of self-sufficiency, materialism and pluralism?

On the one hand, the growth and energy of the church of the South presents the Western church with the question: "How can our relationships and partnerships with Christians from the South be a tool of God to help reinvigorate the church in our postmodern society?" Might the future of short-term missions from the West be more to expose our people to the Acts-like expansion of the church in Southern locales rather than to "do" crosscultural ministry?

On the other hand, our geographical focus for missions will be challenged. What will be our response to Oswald J. Smith's famous quote—"No one should hear the gospel twice before everyone has heard it once"—when the "twice" people are from Nigeria or Brazil or the Philippines, and the "have not heard it once" people are down the street?

A movie: *While You Were Sleeping.* The great value of Jenkins's book is that it reminds us that the world is changing right under our noses. Whether one agrees with his conclusions or even all his data, his book is a wake-up call to the Western church to see the world as it *really* is, not merely as we'd like it to be.

One vivid illustration in this regard is Jenkins's observation about immigration and its impact on Western nations. A few of us are paying attention to the crosscultural world at our doorstep, but for most mission agencies, recruits are still primarily those of European descent who are being trained to go "over there." This represents what David Bosch called the "myth of salt water": it's not missions until we cross a body of salt water.

Does the changing ethnic face of the historical sending nations call us to a radical redefinition of what mission is, especially of the crosscultural variety? The so-called emerging generation grows up in this diverse world, and they look incredulously at the mission recruiter who implies that all of the real needs are "over there." Should every mission focused on reaching out to Africans, Asians or Latin Americans on their continents also train and recruit for a similar outreach to Africans, Asians and Latin Americans *here*?

This wake-up call is especially relevant regarding future missionaries. If Jenkins is correct—that the vast majority of new immigrants to the United States are already Christians—then how will we who mobilize in missions reach out and equip these already crosscultural and often multilingual Christians to the global mission of the church?

An email I received from Torli Krua, a Boston-area Christian worker, spoke to this issue. Torli considers himself to be "an African missionary brought to the United States by a civil war in Liberia." Concerning immigrants and refugees in North America, he writes, "When I look at the immigration problem facing refugees and immigrants and the opportunity for reaching the world by reaching those uprooted by wars who now live at the doorsteps of the church in North America, I see opportunities of collaboration in reaching the world."[3]

A song: *Who Let the Dogs Out?* Here I'm referring to "dogs" in the New Testament sense of heretics or those who distort the gospel. In his analysis of Southern Christianity, Jenkins quickly notes that much of the growth in these regions comes with new forms of indigenous church movements that may or may not adhere to our Western statements of faith. Their localized theologies may be fraught with syncretism and what we in the West consider "heresies." But Jenkins later points out that our more conservative, biblical literalist brothers and sisters in the South may be the ones calling *us* the heretical "dogs," because our faith has succumbed to secularism and modernity.

What will these issues mean in our theological and missiological training? Shall we adapt a Gamaliel-like approach that lets the indigenous church work things out and gravitate back to adherence to the biblical, historical faith? Or shall we work together so that each of our localized perspectives serves to refine the other?

No one in missiological leadership will contest that immense global changes lie ahead. A careful read of Jenkins, however, exhorts us to action so that we in the West are not left behind. It awakens us to new data that will affect our future priorities. And it exhorts us all to globally relevant biblical examination.

2

An Appraisal of the
North American Church

When I travel, my international hosts sometimes ask, "What's America like?" I respond with another question: "Which America are you asking about?" Los Angeles is quite different than Fargo, North Dakota. The cultures of south Boston and south Texas vary greatly.

I offer a similar response to the question, "What's the North American church like?" Which North American churches? The megachurches of Atlanta? The rural churches in northern Maine? Churches in Manitoba, known as the "Bible belt" of Canada? Churches made up of people of European descent or Asian descent or Latino descent or African descent?

And if the question goes to the specific topic of this book—namely, involvement in global mission—the answers will come back equally diverse. One church describes their missional outreach exclusively as outreach to the immediate community. Another gives 30 percent of its total budget to overseas crosscultural ministries. A third is sending people on short-term missions. Yet another gives its entire mission budget to ministries in the countries of origin of its immigrant attendees.

All of this is to illustrate the challenge of trying to write a chapter on the North American church. The title of a recent book—

American Christianities—reminds us that the North American church is not a single unit.[1] Having said all this, I do believe that we can observe certain things about North American churches that relate to our topic: mission in a globalized world. Some congregations have a historic interest in the topic, because of a long and storied past of involvement in crosscultural and international missions. These churches are wondering "What now?" and "What's next?" because they know the nature of global mission is changing. Others are newer churches that realize that the gospel calls every Christian to some form of global involvement: witness or compassion or justice. This, plus the awareness that Majority World churches are growing and sending missionaries to us, has awakened these churches to that fact that global relevance demands global involvement. These churches are looking for effective ways to be involved and steward their people and resources.

Still other churches have started with crosscultural realities at their doorsteps in the form of ethnic minority churches, large immigrant populations or ministries to refugees. These multiple cultures are calling churches to involvement in the world beyond the United States and Canada as they look for ways to connect local ministries to global realities.

With these churches and their members in mind, consider the strengths and weaknesses (or challenges) of the North American church.

North American Church Strengths
It is easy to identify our weaknesses and failures, but let's start with strengths. Consider five.

1. Generosity and economic wealth. Bishop Hwa Yung of Malaysia, in an article titled "A Fresh Call for U.S. Missionaries," notes that the American church is still the largest source of funding for global missions. At the Third Lausanne Congress on World Evangelization in 2010, for example, some 80 percent of the sixteen to seventeen million dollars raised came from Americans.[2] David Ro echoes this theme when he writes, "Financially generous giving is ingrained in Western Christian culture."[3]

Money is not the answer to completing the Great Commission or to empowering the Majority World church, but it is a resource that the church in North America can use. Historically, the North American church has demonstrated great desire to invest in global missions. If that trend continues and we exercise our generosity wisely, finances are one way that we can be part of the advance of the globalized mission of God.

One caveat: there are times when our Western generosity is not accompanied by forethought and evaluation. We do at times give on impulse, a negative side effect of our cultural optimism (see below), and without evaluating strategic impact. With this in mind, books like *When Helping Hurts: How to Alleviate Poverty Without Hurting the Poor . . . and Yourself* can help us learn wisdom in our global giving.[4]

2. Optimism and the belief that change is possible. Over the years, I have had the privilege of asking the questions behind this book to dozens of leaders in the Majority World church. My most common question has been something along the lines of, "Where does the North American church fit in God's global plan?" or "What do we in the North American church bring to the global church table?"

Peter Kuzmič of Croatia, a well-traveled theologian and missiologist, once answered: "naïve optimism." I asked him to explain, because his reply sounded critical, if not derogatory. He noted that our North American heritage combined with our affluence, especially in the United States, has made us optimistic, future-looking and change-oriented. "So many of the more traditional cultures are stuck in the past, fighting old wars and disbelieving in the possibility of change. But North America is all about change and hope and new ideas and innovation."[5]

But what about the naïve part? Peter explained that our zeal for change makes us naïve about the complexities in other cultures (I'll discuss this more later in this chapter). He observed that we in North America tend to oversimplify problems, underestimate the need for careful attention to history and, as a product of our affluence and materialism, believe that money is the key to solving almost any problem. Combined with careful listening and patience, however, the North American "can do" spirit is an essential part of the global church, he explained. In *The New Shape of Global Christianity*, Mark Noll makes a similar point. He says that the North American impact on global Christianity has been largely because of our past emphasis on promoting individual conversion, recruiting a zealous voluntary force and encouraging an entrepreneurial approach.[6]

Vishal Mangalwadi's biography of British missionary William Carey (1761-1834) as a transformer of India focuses on his optimism, which was driven by a Christian worldview. Although not from North America, Carey came to India with a Western "change-for-the-better" worldview that contrasted the karmic worldview, which taught people to accept their lot in life and change nothing. Carey taught that positive change was possible. You don't need to be illiterate anymore. You don't need to suffer with curable diseases. Widows do not need to be cremated alive with their deceased husbands. Mangalwadi writes: "One of the results of Carey's success has been that, since his day, most Indians (including even those who believe in *kārma*, reincarnation, astrology, Brahmanical scriptures, etc.) now tend to agree that reform is possible. They are forced to reject the fatalistic idea that reform is not possible. That premise had ruled Indian civilization and ruined India for two thousand years. Carey's belief that human suffering can be and should be resisted has dominated the last two hundred years of Indian history."[7]

3. Experience in and resources for training. One of the greatest areas in which Majority World leaders are asking for North American involvement is in the area of training and education. Our libraries, seminaries, training institutions, books and trained faculty are viewed as a tremendous resource to the Majority World church.

David Ro grew up as the son of a Korean father and a Chinese mother who served crossculturally in Taiwan and East Asia as missionaries. David has now served with his wife, Jackie, in East Asia for more than a decade. He wrote these reflections to me in an email, "With all its weaknesses, the strengths of the North American church are often downplayed. Here's where I've observed where we can contribute most to the global church: *Theological and biblical depth*: the seminaries, theologians, biblical scholarship is unmatched. *Christian literature* produced in North America by far surpasses any other region or culture. *Global leadership*: it is still only the Western church leaders that can lead a global movement . . . Africans lead Africans, Asia leads Asians, Koreans lead Koreans, Chinese lead Chinese, . . . but Western leaders are still best at leading global international movements like Lausanne. The West is still at the center of global strategic vision and leadership training and thinking."[8]

4. *Multiculturalism.* As I write this word, I can think of a dozen stories of racism, ethnocentric violence and cultural separation in North America, including the sad separation of peoples on Sunday mornings that I mentioned earlier. Nevertheless, North America illustrates to the rest of the world that we can move together toward a multicultural future. Canada probably leads the way over the United States here, but the world took notice in 2008 when the U.S. elected our first-ever African American president. Newspapers around the world after the election featured editorials claiming that what happened in the United States could never happen in their country. They looked at us and asked how a minority-culture person could be elected as leader of the greatest nation on earth (their language, not mine). Although this multiculturalism is more a reflection of North American culture than of the North American church in particular, it is a characteristic on which the church can build.

We still have a long way to go as North American nations and as churches in this regard, but in the multicultural world ahead of us, the lessons we've learned and the mistakes we've made could benefit the church around the world.[9]

5. *History.* Someone once described an expert as a person who has

made every possible mistake and tried to learn from them. In this regard, it is possible that the history of crosscultural mission over the last two hundred years has rendered North American experts. We've made (and are still making) the mistake of bringing too much of our Western cultures with us as we have gone out to serve. Bishop Hwa Yung encourages the North American church to keep sending missionaries. Referring to our history, he celebrates the courageous Westerners who went out to serve in mission. "Many missionaries are remembered with deep affection in the countries they served, for the way they sacrificially brought the gospel," Yung writes. "They went as evangelists and pastors, teachers and professors, doctors and nurses, agriculturalists and engineers. Many died in strange lands but have not been forgotten by those whose lives were changed forever by the message of Christ. There is little doubt that in sheer numbers and overall impact, the American church was the dominant force in foreign missions in the 20th century."

Yung then observes that we are sometimes discouraged to engage with the crosscultural global church because of our past mistakes: "The mistakes—the Crusades, the European wars of religion, and colonial expansion, plus slavery and related issues—have created tremendous angst in the minds of many Americans. When the mistakes of Western missions are thrown into the mix, the guilt complex becomes a potent brew, contributing to the partial loss of nerve in Western missions." But he exhorts us to see our desire to learn from history as a powerful reflection of the gospel itself: "Thus, the Western guilt complex properly understood is also a profound call to humble confidence and boldness in mission."[10] In other words, our capacity to repent and learn from our historical mistakes is itself a resource to help us find our place in global Christianity. Perhaps our awareness of our own historical mistakes—such as cultural imperialism and leading by power rather than by serving—will help us partner with the new missionary senders from Latin America, Africa and Asia. Perhaps they can avoid repeating our mistakes.

North American Church Concerns: Global Issues

When Paul delineated his various sufferings for the sake of the gospel to the Corinthians, he concluded by turning from the outward pressures to his inward stress over the state of the church: "Besides everything else, I face daily the pressure of my concerns for all the churches" (2 Cor 11:28).

As one involved in international ministry as well as in the mobilization of others in the North American church for global prayer and involvement, I identify with this double-sided sense of pressure. Externally, I ache for the church around the world: suffering in Sudan, opposition in Indonesia, people struggling to survive in Iraq. But my internal stresses, the concerns that sometimes keep me awake at night, often relate to the church in my own country and region. As I think about the North American church and our role in world evangelization, I grow increasingly troubled.

Although we might deeply desire collaboration with our sisters and brothers from the Majority World in the ongoing global mission of God, there are more than a few concerns that can derail our involvement. I'll break my concerns into global issues and local issues. Let's start with three global issues. These are the issues that we in the North American church need to wrestle with if we are going to serve the purposes of God in this globalized world.

1. Pluralism: Is Jesus really the only way to God? For those of us old enough to remember, mission conferences of the past were often defined by the singing of "We've a Story to Tell to the Nations." Despite the obvious tones of Western imperialism in the song, it did reflect a core conviction that Jesus Christ is the way, the truth and the life, and the idea that no one could find salvation without a personal response to his love.[11]

The spirit of this age doesn't necessarily accept this belief. The impact of postmodern relativism has left many North American Christians wondering, "Do we *really* have a story to tell to the nations?" Timothy Tennent cites "growing skepticism about the certainty of knowledge" as one of the global megatrends shaping the future of global missions.[12]

In the classes I teach about global Christianity at Gordon College, a Christian liberal arts institution, more than a third of my students do not believe or are uncertain that people outside of Jesus Christ are truly lost. And these are students with a predefined interest in global missions.

Pluralism is perhaps the greatest theological challenge facing the church in North America. Tim Dearborn, writing in "Christ, the Church, and Other Religions" states it this way: "Every local church—whether in Kansas City or Kinshasa, in Toledo or Tokyo, in London or in Latvia—will serve in a religiously pluralistic environment."[13] Pluralism is not a philosophy reserved for the classrooms of Ivy League universities; it is now the dominant worldview of the common person in North America.

The idea that Jesus Christ and Christian faith are unique, a basic motivation for global missions, is far from acceptable in a world that responds to questions of truth with "all of the above." The spirit of the age militates against the proclamation that there is no other name by which we can be saved (see Acts 4:12).

In the worldviews and religions of the East, truth gets absorbed into the pot in which all melt into the composite whole. I once interacted with a woman in Delhi, India, who was registering us for a conference being hosted by her school. Her desk was covered with various pictures of Jesus. I asked, "Are you a follower of Jesus?" Oh yes, she answered; "He is one of my favorites."

"One of my favorites" fits well in the world of Hindu's some three hundred million gods, but it is antithetical to the gospel. It forces the question: are we truly convinced of the uniqueness of Christ, or is he simply our favorite, based on our culture, experience or upbringing?

In the West, pluralism resists any concept of absolute truth. The proponents of pluralism include people like Paul Knitter, who sees every world religion as having saving grace in itself. Others, like Karl Rahner, identify those outside of Christian faith as "anonymous

Christians," saved by Jesus' death and atonement whether they acknowledge him or not.[14]

But most are not as theologically sophisticated as these. Many of us in North America simply absorb a more passive form of pluralism. While we might never say that Jesus is just "one way among many to reach God," our lack of passion for missions and evangelism reflects a theology that Robertson McQuilkin calls the "wider hope" theory: we believe that people who have never heard of Jesus will be saved somehow, without our involvement as evangelists or missionaries.[15]

The pluralistic spirit of the age challenges the very *raison d'être* of mission in a globalized world. If Jesus is not the only way, how does that affect our desire to go to dangerous, difficult places and into hardship situations? In the face of global pluralism, the church must proclaim Jesus Christ with theological integrity, critical contextualization and countercultural preaching.

Pluralism forces us to evaluate our own beliefs and those of others. Do we really understand the beliefs and worldviews of other religions? Are we clear on the differences in what we believe so that we can engage others in dialogue? (As a side note, I'm amazed at the number of churches that, although shocked by the attacks of September 11, 2001, and the subsequent wars, have yet to offer any indepth courses on Islam. If the daily news is not a wake-up call to understand the world's fastest growing religion, what will stir us?)

Tim Dearborn, writing in "Christ, the Church, and Other Religions," observes, "Without a basic comprehension of other's beliefs, our encounters will be characterized by prejudice, paternalism, and pride."[16] Pluralism challenges our skills at ecumenical or interreligious interaction: are we ready to engage people from other faiths like Paul did on Mars Hill? Can we, like Paul, quote from their texts, allude to their philosophies and present Jesus as the answer they are looking for?[17]

When Rob Bell, the dynamic speaker and founder of Mars Hill Bible Church, released his book *Love Wins: Heaven, Hell, and the*

Eternal Fate of Every Person Who Ever Lived, the publishers arranged for multiple speaking tours, including interviews on several national television shows produced in New York City. In one interview on MSNBC, interviewer Martin Bashir, who had obviously read and researched the book carefully, grilled Bell on his statements that challenge the assumptions of traditional evangelical theology regarding heaven, hell and the uniqueness of Jesus.

Again and again the interviewer pushed Bell with the question, "Does a person's decision in this life regarding Jesus Christ have eternal implications in the next?" Again and again Bell tried to redirect the conversation.

Whether you think that Bell waffled or that Bashir was too aggressive, the interview stands as a parable of the Western church versus the Majority World church. Rob Bell is a graduate of Wheaton College and Fuller Theological Seminary, and he is the founder of a suburban megachurch. In his book and in the interview, he dances with pluralism and the implication that a relationship with Jesus might not be necessary for entrance to heaven and avoidance of hell. Perhaps there are other ways to be saved.

The interviewer, Martin Bashir, is not only a well-respected journalist; he is a representative of the Majority World church. Although he interviewed Bell as a careful journalist, Bashir is also from Pakistan and a follower of Jesus converted from Islam. Bashir was the one defending orthodox theology, referring to councils from Christian history and pointing out Bell's direction away from evangelical teaching.

The interview provokes the question: who are now the defenders of the faith? As we in the West deviate, will it be believers in the church in the Majority World who bring us back? Philip Jenkins observes that it is the Christian immigrant populations in Europe, not the native European Christians, who are proclaiming the historic message of salvation through Christ alone. Will the church in North America go the same direction?

2. Globalization: Do we understand the scope of the challenge? What does Christianity look like in a world deeply affected by multinational companies and the Golden Arches? And in the realm of crosscultural mission, what does it mean to be part of the world's largest nonwhite, non-Western religion?

Philip Jenkins points out that, "Over the past century . . . the center of gravity in the Christian world has shifted inexorably southward, to Africa, Asia, and Latin America. Already today, the largest Christian communities on the planet are to be found in Africa and Latin America."[18] David Barrett states that as of 2000, only 39 percent of the world's 1.5 billion Christians live in the industrialized West. Barrett further predicted that by 2025, fully 70 percent of Christians will live in Asia, Africa, Latin America and Oceania.[19]

Globalization has fostered dramatic changes in immigration, urbanization and technological connectivity. The result is that traditional sending structures and the geographic orientation that have dominated missions since the nineteenth century are no longer tenable. The global church exists in an increasingly globalized world. Sociologist George Ritzer describes the loss of local culture at the hands of a homogenizing totality as "the McDonaldization of society."[20]

This globalization leads to what Roland Robertson calls "the compression of the world," a phenomena that has the potential to bring people together, but will just as likely lead to more fragmentation and conflict.[21] In the twenty-first century the rest of the world, while affected by Coca-Cola, satellite communication, Apple, Microsoft and globally interconnected economies, is not melding into some sort of unified whole. Samuel Huntington points to almost a dozen "clashing civilizations," but he predicts that three will predominate: "The dangerous clashes of the future are likely to arise from the interaction of Western arrogance, Islamic intolerance, and Sinic [Chinese] assertiveness."[22]

We serve a global church with a global commission in a globalized world. What will it mean? Will our North American citizenships hurt us or help us? A brother in Zimbabwe reminded me, "What you in the West call 'globalization' we call 'Americanization.'" Can we use the advances of global technology without getting sucked into the exportation of Western materialism? How can we in the Western church serve effectively in a world exploited by our own greed? Can we present the gospel without taking stronger stands against sweatshops, fighting child labor and defending the defenseless?

3. Territorialism: Are we prepared to serve in a hostile world? Clashing civilizations and the resistance to Westernization has fueled a renewed nationalism in many places. And this nationalism is often attached to religion, whether it is nationalistic Buddhism in Sri Lanka, Sharia Islam in northern Nigeria, nationalistic Orthodoxy in the former Communist-bloc countries or Christianity that wraps Bibles in the flag in the United States. Territorialism provides us with a challenge regarding how to relate to the Other; as such, it presents us with the greatest anthropological challenge.

Local war and global peace lead to, according to the title of one book, *Jihad* [religious, often ethnically defined, war] *versus McWorld* [globalization]."[23] In just the last two decades, we have witnessed what happens when ethnic-specific religion declines into little more than tribalism and racism, whether it is the deaths of hundreds of thousands in Rwanda and Burundi, or the Serbian Orthodox-Croatian Catholic-Bosnian Muslim massacres or the often-unnoticed clashes in the Democratic Republic of Congo.

"The lines of conflict are no longer as clear and simplistic as they were during the Cold War," Tim Dearborn writes. "*Battle lines are now drawn between balkanized neighborhoods.*"[24] Peter Kuzmič, who witnessed the atrocities of territorialism firsthand during the Bosnian-Serbian-Croatian crisis of the 1990s, concluded a course he taught on clashing civilizations in this way: religion is back, it is back in big and destructive ways and the United States is increasingly out of touch.

These realities force us to deal with long-term territorial hatreds that never appear in our crosscultural training manuals. The 1994-1995 genocides in Rwanda and Burundi remind us that we must seek to make disciples, not just converts, and that these disciples must grow in understanding Jesus' mandate to love and forgive enemies. The disciple in a territorialized world must not only be taught to look upward to Jesus but also outward to the Other, whom Jesus loves. In this regard, we in the West will need to enter first as learners, not as teachers. How does Christian discipleship help people deal with, in Donald Schriver's words, "the leftover debris of their national pasts"?[25] This "debris" includes ethnic loyalties, religious conflict and an uncrossable memory barrier about "what your people did to my people." It also includes literal "debris." In Bosnia, for example, it included the destruction of forty Orthodox churches, three hundred Roman Catholic churches and over one thousand Muslim mosques.

Many of us come from a cultural context in which we think little about the past: we who are white in the United States seldom want to deal with the lingering legacies of slavery, racism or ethnic cleansing of the indigenous people who were here before European colonization. Until we start wrestling with our collective histories, we won't know how to address the historical hostilities we find elsewhere.

History can also urge us to preach reconciliation with greater resolve. In light of the fantastic progress of Pentecostalism in the world, I've often reminded Pentecostal leaders of their own roots concerning the signs of the Holy Spirit. William Seymour, a key figure in the Azusa Street revivals that birthed the modern Pentecostal movement, came to believe, according to Harvey Cox, that "the truest sign of the presence of the Holy Spirit was not speaking in tongues but the demise of racial barriers between Christians."[26] Tribalism challenges us to build disciples who know how to break down the "dividing walls of hostility" through Christ and thus create the "one new humanity" community of Ephesians 2:15.

North American Church Concerns: Local Issues
In the context of these global challenges, what are the localized, specific

issues that the church from North America faces? Consider these eight.
1. *Ecclesiology.* What is the role of the local church in the sending
process? In the church in North America, I observe an "all or nothing"
phenomenon in response to global missions. Some churches, overwhelmed and "globophobic," choose to do little or nothing. Small
budgets, survival mentalities and local challenges predominate. The
do little/do nothing perspective was summed up by one pastor serving
in a community struggling with an unemployment rate exceeding 22
percent. He told me, "I can scarcely do enough to serve the needs in
my own congregation, and you want me to think about *the world?*"

At the other extreme are those who increase their involvement in
missions, implying or directly stating that they want to return to the
Antioch model *where they do it all.* They want to take back [i.e., from
agencies or denominations] the local church's priority position in the
Great Commission. Ian Douglas observes that this increased involvement and ownership has been made possible by globalization: "We
must recognize that the local churches' ability to connect with other
Christian communities around the world is, in and of itself, a manifes-
tation of the realities of global communication and transportation."[27]

Rick Warren, one of America's best-known pastors, reflects this "do
it all" mentality when he writes: "In the first century, mission strategy
was always congregationally based. . . . Local churches accepted the
responsibility for Jesus' Great Commission and his Great Commandment." Today, Warren writes, he sees that most local churches
have become "sidelined and uninvolved" because the agencies are
saying, "pray, pay and get out of the way." Warren challenges his
readers: "I believe the proper role for all the great parachurch and relief
organizations is to serve local churches in a supportive way, offering
their expertise and knowledge, but allowing local churches around the
world to be the central focus and the distribution centers."[28]

While I zealously endorse a central role for the local church in
God's mission in the world, I wonder what the world will look like
when, rather than ten or twenty or thirty agencies working in com-

petition to evangelize a country or a city, we have hundreds of Western sending churches all creating their own strategies for one locale. In this regard, Todd Johnson observes,

Perhaps the most significant development is the rise of specifically nonglobal plans. Without centralized planning, agencies and churches are focusing more on specific peoples, countries, and regions. Except for the largest agencies [and churches], most work in thirty or fewer countries. As churches begin to work directly on the field, their emphasis is not global but local. The advantage of this type of strategy is the availability of far more resources for reaching unreached peoples. The disadvantage, which has already been observed in places like the former Soviet Union, is massive duplication of resources. What happens when thousands of individuals, churches, and agencies all have their eye on the same new opportunity?[29]

What will the scenario of local church involvement in the future look like? Ian Douglas paints a picture that many of us have lived:

A local congregation here in the United States makes a connection with Christians on the other side of the world through a variety of circumstances—a Tanzanian seminarian studying in the United States begins to worship in the parish, an elder traveling on business in Malaysia find his way into a church in Kuala Lumpur one Sunday morning, or a high school student learns about an Evangelical crusade in Buenos Aires while she surfs the Web. Before you know it there are real and tangible links established between the local parish in the United States and a Christian community in Tanzania, Malaysia, or Argentina. Letters and e-mails are exchanged; building projects are begun with funding from the United States; short-term mission trips for American youth groups are undertaken; doctors, teachers, and technical workers from the United States offer themselves for extended missionary service; and, on occasion, the church leader from Tanzania, Malaysia, or Argentina will travel to the United States, often exchanging pulpits with American pastors.[30]

In summary, global communications, short-term mission travel and the arrival in North American schools, seminaries and churches of Majority World Christian leaders have dramatically reduced the distance between local churches and what used to be called "the field." The net result is more churches attempting to devise their own global initiatives, send their own missionaries and maintain their own partnerships in other countries. While the churches that focus on one locale and stay focused may report good outcomes, other churches may simply repeat the mistakes of North American missionaries of the past.

2. *Disconnectedness with the poorer world.* I've referred already to the rich-poor gap and to mission in a violent world, but hear the challenge again. In a volume dedicated to understanding the role of the local church in a global world, World Vision leaders pointed out that, "While global wealth increased by 40 percent in the 1990s, more than one billion people fell into even deeper poverty. In 1997, the combined income of the 447 wealthiest people in the world was greater than the combined income of 50 percent of the world's population."[31]

The rich-poor gap presents us with many challenges. How can Western missionaries be prepared to go to the poorest, most hostile areas of the world when our lifestyle adjustment is so severe? Can a generation raised on lattes costing three dollars per cup be effective in a world where millions have no access to clean drinking water? Can Westerners who routinely spend eight to twelve dollars to see a movie live effectively alongside the one billion abjectly poor people living on less than one dollar per day? In our techno-driven worlds of Twitter, smartphones and Facebook, how will Westerners respond to living in places that are technologically undeveloped? I've been in locations in northeast India where there was no cellular reception of any kind. In a guest house in one African nation, I asked the desk attendant if they had wireless. "Yes," he replied. "We have no wires." Can a generation accustomed to instant messaging make the adjustment? The rich-poor gap challenges our commitment to incarnational living. We will need to adapt simpler lifestyles *before we go,* to live with diminished material expectations in an effort to increase incarnational effectiveness. And the entire church, so accustomed to spending huge sums on their own comforts and conveniences, must be reawakened to increased generosity and sacrifice.[32]

3. Lack of information. In a discussion with a lay leader at our local church, I referred to a Palestinian Christian friend who serves as a pastor in Old Jerusalem. The lay leader interrupted, "That's impossible; all Palestinians are Muslims." His message to me? *I have my mind made up: don't confuse me with the facts.* This person has a doctorate.

Don't get me wrong. Information-rich individuals are adopting people groups, studying the "Isa Mosque" phenomena or examining indigenous missions. But the vast majority, it seems—the "information poor"—don't know much about global realities. At a seminar with mission and church leaders, for example, we dug into the nuances of Islam, the interpretations of the Koran and the tensions between Christians and Muslims in the world today. But one Sunday at church, I met another lay leader who, in his own words, "couldn't tell you the first thing about what a Muslim believes."

Even sadder was my experience at a mission conference when the associate pastor prayed for the short-term mission team headed to Russia: "Lord, guide them in their evangelistic efforts in *Romania.*" The mission team leader (an excited, globally informed Christian) lamented to me that the pastor did not know that Russia and Romania are different countries!

Consider the relative geographic ignorance of people in the United States (I cannot speak for Canada), and you'll understand the magnitude of the problem. In June 2000, *National Geographic* stated that one in seven adults in the United States could not find our country on a map of the world. Before September 11, many would not have known where Afghanistan is. Peter Kuzmič of Croatia will tell you that most cannot identify the Baltic Republics from the Balkans, and Zac Niringiye of Uganda tells of American pastors asking, "What is the capital of Africa?" Kuzmič reported that in the mid-1990s, during the height of the conflicts in the former Yugoslavia, one-third of the members of the United States Congress had never served in the military or held a passport. Those elected to make decisions on national involvement in international issues had nothing but textbook knowledge of the world.

4. *A propensity to oversimplify the world.* We often talk about Chinese and Muslims and Hindus and Latinos—or even "the West"—as if these words represent large, homogeneous units. With such an oversimplified view of cultures (and the multiple cultures within cultures), it is no wonder that church leaders fall prey to global plans designed to "crack the code" of a culture and evangelize everyone at once through a campaign, a movie or a technique.

5. *A propensity to nationalize God.* In this category, I write primarily to my fellow United States citizens. World events over the last twenty years have exaggerated our propensity to blur the lines between nationalistic fervor and Christian faith. We in the United States tend to talk about deaths in wars as if only "our side" counts. We pray prayers identifying "us" versus "them," with the obvious implication that God must be on our side. We sing "God Bless America" at sporting events and then wonder why Muslims in the Middle East conclude that we are calling on our God against theirs.

Christians in the Muslim world warn us that the blurring of these Christian and nationalistic lines will confirm to some Muslims the need for "holy war." These Christians tell us that identifying our Christianity with American foreign policy may only intensify the commitments of some Muslims to the idea of jihad. They urge us to remember that our first citizenship is in heaven!

6. *Failure to think critically.* I wonder if we in the church have lost our ability to think critically. The church speaks as God's prophetic

voice, but have we become so "amused to death" (*a-muse* means "no thinking") that we simply absorb the status quo?[33]

Consider our ability to think critically about where we've been and to learn from history. Present an American pastor with the historical perspective of a Palestinian, who believes that land his or her family has occupied for over one thousand years was stolen from them, and you'll be labeled an apostate. Or how about our ability to think critically about what we're doing? I am a devoted advocate of short-term missions, but is it possible that the idea needs some serious review? Many churches seem to believe that the global cause of Christ will automatically follow our increase in short-term missions, or they condition their financial support of missionaries or agencies based on the missionaries' or agencies' willingness to host the church's short-term mission efforts. Doing more and involving more people takes the priority, without much evaluation of the local, financial and global impact.

Patrick Johnstone, one of the most knowledgeable people on earth concerning global Christianity, recently identified four priorities facing the Western church in the next forty years. Number three on his list is, "The limitations and costs of short-term missions need to be watched, and all short-term programs evaluated for their value-added contribution to the overall goal of world evangelization."[34]

Is anyone thinking critically about where we're going? When churches hear the presentation of some mission agencies, they can get the impression that the replacement of retiring Western missionaries is the highest priority in world evangelization. Are we assuming that Western missionary influence needs to stay the same or increase? Other presentations seem to imply that indigenous leaders will do all that remains of the work of world evangelization. All we need to do is send our checks while we stay home and wax our cars.[35]

We who lead the mission endeavors of local churches must be willing to blend our enthusiastic optimism with willingness to be more self-critical. We must devote ourselves to serious listening to our non-Western counterparts (the second section of this book is an attempt to help us get started at this). Without critical thinking, we'll simply repeat the errors of the past or launch ourselves into global isolation.

7. *Option overload.* The intensification of program-driven church ministries inevitably shoves global issues into a category one pastor calls "sideshow missions." Other priorities drive the church, and missions and world concern get shoved to the periphery. Some devotees will faithfully carry the burden (and attend the midweek program), but most see missions as one option among many. Often the music ministry or men's ministry or hundreds of other specialized ministries will keep people from involvement in the wider world.

With all due respect to those who experience the actual disorder, I sometimes wonder if we in the church don't have a case of global attention deficit disorder. We participate in missions with a remote control in our hands. Today is the fundraiser for the seminary in Brazil, tomorrow the one for the short-term mission trip to Burkina Faso. The guest speaker represents indigenous missionaries from India, and the Sunday school–adopted missionary translates the Bible in Southeast Asia. We move freely from project to project and place to place with little concern for long-term issues.

We might critique the church in other parts of the world as being a mile wide and an inch deep, but I wonder if our missions programs in the North American church don't have the same malady. If we do have a case of global attention deficit disorder, how will our hesitancy to make long-term commitments minimize our effectiveness? How will our distraction affect our outreach to Muslims, Hindus and others, who might require years of relationship and service before they consider Jesus?

Several years ago, I met with recruiters for Wycliffe Bible Translators to discuss the mobilization of new missionaries. They asked this basic question: do those coming out of the United States church have the focus, commitment and sacrifice necessary to do the work of Bible translation? I didn't know what to tell them, except that I wonder too.

The writers of *Missional Church: A Vision for the Sending of the Church in North* America, call readers to see the church "not as the purpose or goal of the gospel, but rather as the instrument and witness" of the mission of God *(missio Dei)* in the world. They write: "In the ecclesiocentric approach of Christendom, mission became only one of the many programs of the church . . . it has taken us decades to realize that mission is not just a program. It defines the church as God's sent people. Either mission defines us, or we reduce the scope of the gospel and the mandate of the church. *Thus our challenge today is to move from church with mission to missional church.*"[36]

8. Cross-less Christianity? A leader from Southeast Asia wrote an essay several years ago critiquing the American church's excesses in supporting and sending short-term missionaries. He titled the article "Bring Back the Missionary Cross." The theme carries into our lives. What will the missionary cross look like to new North American missionary candidates who bring to crosscultural settings their addiction to comfort? Will those people who demand evacuation policies and send multiple containers full of "stuff" be able to be incarnational ministers of the gospel in the midst of Majority World poverty?

A few years ago, after participating in a mission conference that included over one thousand Nigerian pastors, I wrote in my report their sense of zeal, devotion and reckless abandon to the call of Christ to go and make disciples. I commented on their Abrahamic willingness to go out, not knowing where they are going, and on their Pauline "to live is Christ and to die is gain" attitude toward the hardships ahead. A veteran leader of an agency working among Muslims read my report, and he reflected: "The Nigerians remind me of how older generations went out. Today, I spend hours and hours on evacuation policies, hostage policies, and insurance policies. In the old days, we just went and died."

I wonder what taking up the cross daily will mean for me and my wife. I wonder what it might mean for you. In a world of spiraling violence, clashing civilizations and increased hostilities, will it mean intensified opposition to Christians? As Jesus reminds us, the gospel of the kingdom will be *preached to all nations*, and then the end will come. But we cannot forget that the context of that prediction says first that we will be "hated by all nations" (Mt 24:9). We face a great challenge ahead in living and presenting the way of the cross.

Listening to the Majority World

Given the strengths of the North American church, as well as the global and local issues that might hamper our effectiveness, we need to hear the questions Majority World Christians are asking us.

In his presentation at Orlando 2011, the annual leadership consultation of the Mission America Coalition, Doug Birdsall of the Global Lausanne Movement reported on the three questions that he has heard repeatedly from leaders around the world with respect to the U.S. church. After months of global travel to listening events related to the Cape Town 2010 congress, Birdsall posed these questions to the North American church from the Majority World church.[37]

1. Does the church in America have a prophetic role in its own society, or does it simply mimic the culture and entertain its members? Echoing this concern, Jairus Mutebe writes from Kampala, Uganda: "The place of the North American church in the global church is first and foremost modeling. When the North American church stands up for Christ in the face of growing and infiltrating secularism and compromise, we in the global arena have somebody to emulate and also wave before our dissenters as to the credibility and potency of the gospel."[38]

European mission leader Richard Tiplady adds:

> The first place where North Americans fit in mission is in North America. I still see too much separation between thinking about "missions" (which normally means somewhere else in the world) and "ministry" or "evangelism" locally. The churches of North America face (and will increas-

ingly face) a huge task in bringing the gospel to North America in a way that really transforms communities and society as a whole in line with the values and life of the kingdom. (One small [large!] example: How different would our world be today if there had been effective mission among those who a few years ago felt free to make huge personal fortunes out of subprime mortgages in the United States? The results of the nonevangelization of that segment of American society has today had global outcomes effecting millions of lives.) So, start at home![39]

2. Does the church in America have the humility to learn from us, or do they consider themselves to be the world's teacher?

3. Does the American church have the magnanimous spirit to work alongside us in genuine partnership that is based upon mutual respect and shared resources, or do they simply see us as their "partners" to fulfill their plans in our countries?

How do we respond to these questions? How are we responding? As we ponder these questions and move toward a greater understanding of the Majority World church, we need to hear again the words of the Asian leader I cited earlier: bring back the missionary cross. The way forward (as I'll reiterate later) is the way of the cross, the way of humility and the way of servanthood.

Mission historian Andrew Walls offers us these words of comfort and challenge: "Christian advance is not steady inevitable progress. Advance is often followed by recession. The spread of the gospel does not produce permanent gains that can be plotted on a map: 'We have done that.' Christianity has vulnerability at its very heart, fragility in its expression. It's perhaps the vulnerability of the cross and the fragility of the earthen vessel." Walls continues:

> Christian advance in the world is serial and, in the providence of God, it is the Christians of Africa and Asia and Latin America

and the Pacific that are next in the series. We who belong to the West are no longer the leaders, the initiators, the norm setters. We are now to learn to be the helpers, the assistants and the facilitators. The great event, the great surprise for Christianity over the past hundred years, has been this shift in the center of gravity of the church. This radical change in its demographic and cultural composition, by all present indications, appears to be continuing. It means that the Christians of the southern continents are now the representative Christians, the people by whom the quality of twenty-first- and twenty-second-century Christianity will be judged, the people who will set the norms, the standard Christians. And the quality of twenty-first-century Christianity will depend on them.[40]

What does our analysis of the North American church's strengths and weaknesses, combined with feedback from these global leaders, tell us? In short, there is definitely a place for us in the global mission of God, but we must approach our global family with humility and a commitment to be learners. We'll return to these themes, but first, a look at this amazing worldwide family of Jesus followers to whom we belong.

Questions and Next Steps

1. How do you respond to the concerns about the North American church that this chapter outlines?

2. What concerns would you add to those in this chapter, either regarding your own local fellowship or in the church at large across North America?

3

An Appraisal of the Majority World Church

The Majority World is moving from being a mission field to a mission force. As I've already observed, the present reality of global Christianity involves people from the historical missionary "receiving" nations now becoming "sending and receiving" nations.

In the past decade, I have met Brazilian missionaries serving in Algeria, Egyptians serving in Spain, Filipinos serving in Tibet and Nigerians serving in Morocco. The picture of the Majority World church is a picture moving from everywhere to everywhere through the migrations of peoples, urbanization and the new mission movements.

An overview reveals a global church that is predominantly not from European descent, not materially wealthy, not from the postmodern worldview of the West and often not concerned whether their theology fits into all of the neat and tidy categories of Western thinking.

While many in the Western (or in our case North American) world want to celebrate the coming of global Christianity, many remain at a distance. We either retreat into our old North American paradigms of doing missions or we simply stay home. Neither approach is useful. We need to find ways of not only celebrating their success but also entering together into the global challenge of mission ahead.

Majority World Church Strengths

As I did in the previous chapter, I cite here several of the great strengths of the Majority World church and then express my concerns.

1. Zeal for the Lord. Walk the streets of Manila or Nairobi or Buenos Aires on a Sunday morning—or often at other times during the week—and the loud sound of Christian praise fills the air. With the assistance of sound systems, many of the Majority World's worship services are, in a word, loud. This volume is the result of expressiveness in worship and people crying out in prayer: of desperate worshipers on their faces, beseeching God with a great hunger to know him. They come together to offer their whole selves to God. They pray loudly, sing vigorously and confess emotionally.

In several global worship services, I've thought of David's "leaping and dancing before the LORD" (2 Sam 6:16). This delightful style of worship, characterized by reckless, selfless abandon, is unlike my typical worship experience, which is often subdued, self-conscious and preoccupied with maintaining control.

Our worldwide brothers and sisters are often literally living out the psalmist's words "zeal for your house will consume me" (Jn 2:17). United prayer cries out for God's direction. People listen to the preached word with a sense of anticipation. They celebrate with a wild joy that brings to mind C. S. Lewis's description of Aslan as "not a tame lion."[1] Their worship is not tame. I may be exaggerating—I have seen believers around the world falling asleep in worship services or reading their text messages during the sermon. But the freshness of the gospel and the acute awareness of their reliance on God creates a hunger to know God in the Majority World—a desire that often seems diluted in my culture by the "worries of this life and the deceitfulness of wealth" (Mt 13:22).

One great illustration of this zeal came at the twentieth-anniversary celebration of the Christian Mission Foundation, an indigenous Nigerian mission agency with 259 missionaries serving in ten countries (who have planted over 160 new churches). Every language or ethnic group represented at the conference led in an indigenous song, usually a song related to God's saving power in Jesus Christ. Each song came with accompanying dance, and after several hours of praise, we were literally exhausted, an experience I seldom have in American worship services. (Incidentally, I thank God that they forgot to ask this American to come up front to help lead the dancing!)

The skeptic might ask, "Is it just emotion?" or "Does the emotion expressed in worship gets translated into daily living?" Most Majority World church leaders I've met are acutely aware of and concerned about this danger. This is why, at another conference for university students in Ghana, worship leaders called for times of silent reflection and teachers exhorted Christians to repent and to pursue practical holiness. From my vantage point, I wish that my church and the other Christian gatherings I visit in the United States would have a problem of managing excessive zeal!

2. *Zeal for missions.* We need not travel far into the Majority World church before we start hearing calls to global mission with phrases like "This is our time!" or "No longer a mission field; now a mission force" or "The torch (or baton) of global mission has been passed."

Miriam Adeney offers these vivid illustrations: She reports that in the jungles of Brazil, over one thousand Indians from a dazzling variety of tribes gather annually in conferences to worship and fellowship. In 2008, fourteen hundred delegates convened.[2] Again, she notes that almost ten thousand Spanish- and Portuguese-speaking missionaries serve around the globe.[3] And in Nigeria, Africa's most populous nation, the Nigerian Evangelical Missions Association (NEMA) coordinates a network of more than one hundred Nigerian denominations and organizations. Adeney reports that NEMA now has five thousand two hundred Nigerian missionaries serving in fifty-six countries, and many of these are in places that are hostile to Christians. But their zeal prevails. Adeney writes, "Witness is alive across Africa. If churches are burned, leaders emerge from the fire."[4]

At the Nigeria Fellowship of Evangelical Students' triennial student mission conference, over six thousand students heard speaker after speaker telling them that it is their destiny to take the gospel to the ends of the earth. They sang with great conviction their sense of mission destiny in a song to the tune of "All Hail the Power of Jesus' Name": "Let every believer rise up / To proclaim Christ as Lord / And all Africa shall be saved / To crown him Lord of all."

Mission historian Andrew Walls observes: "Over the past century, Christian advance and Christian recession have gone on simultaneously: recession in the West, advance in Africa, Asia and Latin America; withering at the center, blossoming at the edges. The baton is passing to the Christians of Asia and Africa and the Americas, and . . . the Pacific. . . . But it's in these areas, these southern continents, if we may so call them, where more and more every year responsibility now lies for Christian mission in the world."[5]

Yacob Moussa grew up as a Muslim in Niger. He testifies that he had a sense of destiny and wanted to become a great leader in his nation. He thought that communism was the way, so he went to China to study. In China, he learned that communism is atheistic, so he rejected it because of his Muslim beliefs. But he was disillusioned. In China, a Christian found him and, through testimony, miracles and some dreams, led Moussa to Jesus Christ. Moussa is now doing missions work in Togo, believing that it is God's call to use him to train Togolese to go to his own people back in Niger to preach Jesus Christ. Moussa cannot go himself, because his conversion from Islam might put his life at risk.

I wish you had joined me at a conference related to an African church that gives 80 percent of its budget to crosscultural missions and that works with an African mission-sending agency. You would have heard stories such as:

- A report from Benin that rejoices over fifteen new mission school graduates, that voodoo is being rooted out in the church, that pioneer work is being done among sixteen different ethnic/language groups and that there are eighty-two trainees in the mission's training school.

- A moving report from new believers from the Gambia.

- An appeal for people to go as crosscultural pioneer missionaries to Guinea-Bissau—*for a minimum of fifteen years!*

- A report from ministry within war-torn Liberia.

- A report from the Central African Republic on the work among the pygmies, and an appeal for prayer for a country that calls itself "86 percent Christian" but that has little mission knowledge or commitment.[6]

- Stories ranging from confronting the challenges of Islam in the north; churches being planted; work among students; and the training of thousands of midwives as part of an ongoing commitment to holistic village ministry.

- The commissioning service of missionaries going to new fields like China, Cote d'Ivoire, Tanzania and northern Sudan.

And that's just a sample. Similar reports come out of conferences in Latin America and Asia as well. In *The Church Is Bigger Than You Think,* Patrick Johnstone challenges the reader, "there is a you-shaped hole in God's Kingdom. Find it and fill it."[7] Many of our global Christian family members earnestly desire to understand their unique destiny from God and fulfill it.

Of course, this sense of destiny carries with it the danger of a new form of cultural imperialism: "I've got it and you don't." The new mission force from places like Brazil and South Korea and south India and Nigeria are learning that crosscultural mission work requires patience, language and culture learning, and a leaving behind of some of their own cultural expressions of faith. Nevertheless, the fervor for taking the gospel to all nations provokes us all to greater commitment.

3. Expectancy and faith. When the Christian believers that I've met across the Majority World pray, they really expect God to speak, act, heal and deliver. When they pray for an unreached language or ethnic group, they expect some will be called out to go. They come to prayer expecting that God will work miracles.

At a gathering of believers in one Majority World country (the name is concealed for security purposes), returning missionaries shared stories of how God worked and did miracles and came to people in dreams. Many of the testimonies included stories of signs and wonders, healings and visions and encounters with Muslim or animist spiritual forces. One team celebrated the fact that church planting had gone forward after "four different people were raised from the dead and two warring villages were reconciled."

In much of the global church, we find no debate about whether Mark 16:9-20 appeared in the earliest manuscripts or if the miracles of the first century were "for today." These people live in hardship and environments of blatant spiritual warfare. They don't have our luxury of relegating biblical miracles to Bible times. If the Bible records stories about miracles happening then, they believe miracles can happen *now*. I consistently find my own lack of expectation rebuked.

I am bald. And I live and travel with insulin-dependent diabetes, a disease that requires quite a bit of management, including multiple blood tests and insulin shots every day. When traveling in Africa, Asia and Latin America, my hosts have asked if they can pray for my healing. I welcome it, and they pray. I've been anointed with oil. I've been prayed for at a volume that could have vibrated the diabetes out of me. I've been picked up by a Goliath-size fellow who shook me so hard as he prayed that I thought the disease might fall out of my shoes.

At this writing, God has not chosen to heal the disease miraculously, but I can assure you, it's not from lack of faith. If the faith expressed by my colleagues were the only requirements, my disease would be gone and my hair would have grown back! But my global peers have taught me to pray with expectancy (and if you get diabetes, I'll gladly pray for your miraculous healing!).

4. Rugged, sacrificial faith. Christians from the Majority World almost all go into the world to serve as bivocational workers, sometimes called *tentmakers*. They might go as missionaries, but they run their own Internet cafés, repair cars, farm, do medical work or serve as veterinarians. They are a tough, hardworking lot! When they go out as missionaries or into the ministry, they go expecting hardship and the need to create sources of income for themselves. Many of their testimonies include stories of God's last-minute deliverance with miracles of food or finance or healings or medicine being delivered.

From these brothers and sisters, we learn something of the raw commitment and faith that must have accompanied those first missionaries to Africa in the eighteenth and nineteenth centuries. As I've listened to testimonies from crosscultural workers from places like Indonesia or China or Colombia and heard them pray, I've sensed that I was living in a chapter of the book of Acts from the first century.

One Majority World missionary explained to me, "Brother Paul, where we work we need to have rugged faith. We need to trust God for everything. We need to trust God for petrol to drive our cars. We pray that the electrical power will work. We pray that we will not be robbed on the highway. And when people are sick, we cannot depend on medicine and doctors and clinics like you do. We go to God and cry out for people to be healed." Then he told me the story of the time that his young son had a scrape on his leg that got infected and resulted in a fever. The fever and infection grew in intensity, and they took him to a clinic, but there was no doctor and no medicine. All they could do was pray. They prayed the night through until the fever broke.

An initiative in the house-church movement in China is calling for 100,000 Chinese missionaries to take the gospel across the Buddhist, Hindu and Muslim world and "back to Jerusalem." In their call, the Chinese Christians publicly express their expectation that obeying this call will result in ten thousand martyrdoms. What a contrast to our North American context, in which our first question before we go

is often, "Is it safe there?" While we buy insurance plans with evacuation policies, the Chinese leaders call for a 10 percent martyrdom
rate. Rugged faith indeed!

Majority World Church Concerns

For those of us who live in North America and who begin learning
about the church in other parts of the world, it can be easy to start
thinking, "Our churches are full of problems and the Majority World
church is really getting Christian faith right. We should simply move
out of the way and let them charge ahead."

While I believe that in many situations we need to move out of
the way and let them take the lead, the Majority World church is
far from perfect. In my thirty years of developing relationships
with leaders from Africa, Asia and Latin America, I have met many
beautiful Christians like the people cited earlier. But I have also
met leaders who abuse power, mismanage money and lie about
their ministry success. I've interacted with Christians whose
ethnic identity rules over their Christian identity. I know a deeply
respected Christian leader who (we discovered later) committed
adultery at a global Christian conference that he was helping to
host. In short, I'm both pleased and saddened to report that sin-
fulness knows no cultural or geographic boundaries.

In some situations, the Majority World Christian culture has absorbed some of the worst traits of the missionaries who initially
brought the gospel to them. In other situations, religious or cultural
syncretism has diluted the gospel and led to heresy. The flaws of the
global church always serve as a reminder of the tax collector's prayer:
God have mercy on all of us sinners (Lk 18:13).

For the sake of overview, consider these weaknesses and challenges.

1. Abuse of power. Perhaps it results from the exportation of
Western individualism through colonialist mission endeavors or
from the human inclination to exert power over others. Perhaps the
cause traces back to cultural roots in which people conquered others

and the losers were forced to submit. Whatever the cause, the use of power in leadership, the preoccupation with success and the domination of leaders over followers exists as much in the Majority World as it does in North America. We encounter three indicators of this preoccupation with power wherever we travel.

- *Leaders leading from a platform of power.* You do not need to travel far across the Christian community in Africa, Asia and Latin America before you encounter self-appointed bishops, prophets and apostles. Indigenous churches spring up, led by charismatic leaders who ascribe as much authority (if not more) to their prophetic utterances as they do to the Bible.[8] These leaders often present themselves as infallible. Introduce the idea of servant leadership (as I will later in this book), and you will be identified as weak. Disagree with the founder or the apostle, and you will soon be looking for a new church.

  If one of the characteristics of our North American cultures is individualism, it has often spawned a deeper commitment in ministry and relationships to egalitarian views. In many situations, the consensus of the group is sought so that every person can add something to the conversation or the team or the decision at hand. In contrast, many of the cultures found across the Majority World have a deep respect for things like age, position, titles, heritage and degrees. The down side of this deep respect can be the way that leaders get put on pedestals, creating something that culture specialists call "power-distance."

  The issue I'm addressing here is not the experience of Holy Spirit power. The issue is the abuse of human power, when some claim authority over the lives of others. The abuse can become physical and even sexual. Such abusers are either people who love to manipulate others or else genuine leaders who have allowed God-anointed power to go to their heads, like King Saul did.

- *Leaders who refuse to pass on leadership to others.* The young men and sometimes women who began the indigenous Christian movements in the Majority World were sometimes seen as rebels and revolutionaries in the middle years of the twentieth century. But like their political counterparts, they followed the adage that "today's revolutionary becomes tomorrow's dictator."

It is common across the Majority World to see what is often called "the Big Man" syndrome. These are the leaders who were the pioneers of specific ministries and who now refuse to hand over leadership to others.

- *The explosive growth of denominations.* Leaders who hold on to power and refuse to hand their ministries over to others leave the creative, gifted younger generation little choice. You either submit to the "Big Man" or you depart that ministry and start your own (often getting labeled as "unsubmissive" along the way).

A statistical perspective illustrates this reality. Todd Johnson reports that there are currently 41,000 Christian denominations in 232 countries in the world, ranging in size from millions to fewer than one hundred. He projects that this figure will be 55,000 denominations by the year 2025, with most of the new ones coming out of the Majority World.[9] From some vantage points, the global church seems to be getting more fragmented, like the description of the people of Israel in the age of the Judges, when "everyone did as they saw fit" (Judg 21:25).

2. *Making converts, not disciples.* Again, it is futile here to try to identify where to assign blame—to local cultures themselves, or to Western culture, which exported it in mission—but the Majority World church struggles with the "miles wide, inches deep" problem every bit as much as we do in the West. In some of the areas of the world where the church is new or rising up under the shadows of persecution, the problem might be caused by young and immature church leaders. Miriam Adeney observes that "getting mature pastors in China is a challenge. The two-year-olds are teaching the one-year-olds."[10]

But in the areas where Christianity is free to grow, churches are measured by attendance rather than impact on society. People come to healing and miracle services looking for personal blessings. Bible reading, local witness and the integration of Christian faith into day-to-day life might be nonexistent.

Isaiah Lawon in Ibadan, Nigeria, left the leadership of a church in which he had thirteen thousand regular attendees to launch a new church dedicated to personal, in-depth Christian growth. Why? In his own words: "We had thirteen thousand weekly worshipers, but I had no idea if any of them were becoming disciples."

Church size is not the only issue. Some churches numbering in the tens of thousands have every member in small group account-ability structures. The issue is often unrelated to size. The issue is, borrowing a phrase from Jenkins's *Next Christendom*, that people are drawn to the Christian appeal that our God is "a God you can use," which is the foundation for prosperity theology.

3. *Prosperity theology.* African theologians tell me that this movement came as a result of preachers from North America and Europe in the twentieth century coming with the message of the miracle of "seed faith." Those missionaries would essentially say: "If you give a gift (usually financial) to my ministry, you're planting a seed of faith that you are asking God to multiply five or ten or one hundred times." Accompanying this theology was the promise that enough faith would guarantee healing, new jobs, fertility, success in school and, most significantly, financial prosperity.[11]

When we travel, we are often asked questions such as, "What do you think of [a prosperity-teaching Westerner] who appears on Ma-jority World television or holds crusades across these regions?" The inquirer is seldom asking for critique. He or she wants to tell us the story of a healing that came from touching the television set or a fi-nancial windfall that came after a smaller financial gift.

It is easy for us to critique all this as hyperemotionalism or as crowd manipulation, but the attraction of prosperity teaching makes much more sense when you live in a world of abject poverty. Believers are not just looking for the eternal life to come. They want deliverance from the suffering that is *now*.[12]

On my first trip to Ghana, my long-time colleague Jude Hama of Scripture Union decided to give me the broadest exposure possible to the movements of the church in his country. We visited with Methodist bishops, Baptist leaders and Pentecostal church leaders whose churches were sending missionaries all over the world. We visited Presbyterians, Anglicans and charismatics.

This last church was the most fascinating. The preacher, a man who weighed at least three hundred pounds (although he was only five feet, six inches tall), testified that his physical size was evidence of God's poured-out blessings. As the service progressed, people came and laid their money on the stairs leading up to the stage. At several points, beautifully dressed ladies carrying baskets on their heads would collect the money. And the process would then repeat, and more people would lay more money on the stairs.

Jude explained, "These people have a prayer request: a job, an illness, a desire to marry, etc. The money is their 'love offering' and is designed to let God know that they are serious about their request." Seed faith expressed in Ghana dollars. Jude went on: "You see, Paul, you in America concentrate on the God of love. But here we want the God of *power*. When you live in poverty or with some incurable affliction or some injustice, you don't want to feel loved. You want God's power to make you prosper, or to make you healthy or to make you free. And they have been taught and they believe that money is the way to release the power."

Prosperity theology can be difficult to debunk, because there are often corresponding benefits to turning to greater faithfulness and righteous living. A "hidden sin" could be the reason that a healing request fails or a claim of prosperity goes fruitless. Miriam Adeney writes that the "'prosperity gospel' teachers are partly right. Christian faith often helps the family budget. People get drunk less. Their lives become more orderly. They become more accountable.

Many churches help people in dysfunctional situations. . . .
Christian faith encourages and inspires and motivates. Renouncing
idols and serving Christ blesses individuals and can also bless
communities and nations."[13]

The problem with the prosperity gospel, of course, is that faith is
not a formula or a divine ATM at which the proper code guarantees
a release of funds or health. A colleague in India observed that it is
tragic to see people accept Christ in hopes that he will lead them out
of poverty. When their situation in life does not change, they may
abandon faith, concluding that "trusting Jesus doesn't work." Many
of God's people die of cancer, suffer with diseases and endure lives of
poverty because of cultural, economic or historical factors.

When Jesus is only presented as the "God you can use," what do
we do when God doesn't grant our wishes and petitions? The fallout,
usually eighteen to twenty-four months after entering the "seed
faith" world and being disappointed, can be dramatic.

4. *Ignoring societal transformation.* Perhaps because they have followed in the footsteps of the dualistic world of their missionary fore-
bears, Christians in many parts of the Majority World tend to focus on
the church, fellow believers and the needs of the Christian community.
The society at large gets neglected. Even worse, the Christians who do
enter leadership in the worlds of politics, entertainment and academia
become cultural replications of their secular counterparts.

Obviously, in countries in which Christianity is a tiny percentage
of the whole (or a persecuted minority), societal impact is less possible, although the rise of Christians in the realms of academic influence in China might prove me wrong. But in countries in which
Christianity is a majority, political or business leaders who are
church members and graduates of Christian schools can be just as
corrupt as (or more than) the non-Christians around them.

There could be many reasons for this including poor training, lack
of integrated Christianity or rampant individualism (translated in
some countries as standing only for the rights of my individual

ethnic group). But the church in the Majority World often wants to preach to the poor without actually addressing the structural evils that perpetuate suffering.

All of us—churches both in North America and around the world—are wise to listen to the challenge attributed to the late John Stott. Referring to the parable of the good Samaritan (Lk 10:25-37), Stott observed that the church should not be simply bandaging the wounds of travelers robbed along the Jericho Road. At some point we need to address the structural issues that keep the Jericho Road unsafe.

Moving Ahead

The church around the world contains both strengths and weaknesses, but as Paul wrote to the Colossians, "the gospel is bearing fruit and growing throughout the whole world" (Col 1:6). By the grace of God, our weaknesses do not disqualify us, and by the mercy of God, all of us, as members of God's global church, can move ahead together. Each church and each believer has something to offer, so that we can be part of the answer to the prayer "Thy kingdom come. Thy will be done" (Lk 11:2 KJV).

When we join together—rich and poor, Western and non-Western, brothers and sisters—we can learn how to steward our mutual resources toward the vision of a global family in worship: from every tribe, language, people and nation (Rev 5:9; 7:9).

Questions and Next Steps

1. What did you learn in this chapter about the church in the Majority World?

2. What questions did this chapter raise that you or your small group might want to investigate more?

3. Before you begin the next section, consider what your church, ministry group and household have to offer in partnership with the Majority World church.

Part Two

Moving Forward

With a fast-changing world, a Western church in transition and a growing and often more vibrant Majority World church, we in North America still need to remember our God-given mandate to be involved in the nations. This, combined with our vast human and material resources, makes us stewards of a resource that must be managed carefully. But how do we proceed?

This section is a call to listen, learn, serve and lead together. Throughout this section I'll include stories of constructive, long-term relationships that I have seen work on a global scale. The core issue that we in North America face—especially those of us who represent the presently dominant cultures of the United States and Canada—is similar to the changing overall global self-image of North America, especially the United States. What does it mean to live in what Fareed Zakaria calls a "post-American world"?[1] He summarizes the main idea of his book by that name in the first sentence: "This is a book not about the decline of America but rather about the rise of everyone else."[2] The book jacket describes the challenge to America: "Washington needs to begin a serious transformation of its global strategy, moving from its traditional role of dominating hegemon to that of a more pragmatic, honest broker. It must learn to share power, create coalitions, build legitimacy, and define the global agenda—all formidable tasks."

Much of the same could be said about the North American perspective on global mission. The growth of the global church is not a confirmation of the decline of the North American church but of the rise of everybody else. Recipients are now senders. Those who were once solely a mission field have become a mission force. And the movement of peoples in the world has blurred the lines between the "senders" and the "mission field."

Continuing the parallel with Zakaria's observations about America, the North American mission movement needs a dramatic transformation of our global strategy. Rather than seeing ourselves as brokers, working from the posture of power (which is Zakaria's assumption about America), we need to start seeing ourselves as servants in the global church. We need to learn how to share power, yes, but more realistically we need to learn to release it. We still have a posture from which we can at times build coalitions, but we also need to learn to join coalitions that we did not initiate. We need to join God's global agenda rather than define it.

In short, we need to learn how to participate from a platform of servanthood rather than power. Let me illustrate. In my fifteen years as a global outreach pastor, I observed two types of North American ministries doing global ministry. The first ministry came together, often in North America, and prayerfully asked God for vision for (as a random example) Argentina and how they should initiate their work in Argentina. After developing their vision, they would go to Argentina to recruit Argentine Christians to join their vision.

The recruitment would go something like this: "Jorge, this is our vision for Argentina. Would you join us and help us fulfill our vision—what we believe to be God's vision—for Argentina?" Often Jorge would say yes, especially if the North American mission came fully funded and offered him a decent salary.

The second ministry might also develop a burden for a specific country (let's stick with Argentina), but when they went and visited Jorge, their approach was different. They would say, "Jorge, we believe that God has given us a burden for Argentina, but we're here to serve. What is your vision for Argentina? And is there anything in our experiences or resources that you could use to fulfill your vision for your country?"

Both ministry approaches could have some success, but the former kept the North Americans on the platform of leadership, often dictating the strategy and funding the vision to the point that local leaders became dependent and failed to look for local, indigenous sources of support. This approach could work, especially if it was well funded. But for leaders like Jorge, it was an outsider's plan imposed on his country. After the funding was gone, these ministries often faltered.

The latter approach assigned both dignity and responsibility to Jorge so that the ministry could be sustainable long after the North Americans had departed or the funding had been exhausted. When Christie and I knew that it was time to depart our role as global mission leaders in the church, we joined a small leadership development ministry that followed the second approach: coming alongside the vision of Majority World church leaders to ask if we could assist them in fulfilling their God-given vision. In our first year, we knew we had made the right decision. Through a series of friendships, we had many contacts in Sri Lanka, so we hoped to bring our leadership development training to Sri Lanka. Our organizational president commissioned us to do a "listening trip." Christie and I went to listen to national leaders and to see if we had anything that might help them fulfill their vision for their own country.

We completed meetings with leaders from over a dozen ministries over a ten-day period. Toward the end of our journey, we asked our Sri Lankan host for his feedback. After about the fourth day, he had become convinced that we were actually there to listen, so his feedback was honest. He said (and I'm paraphrasing):

Paul and Christie, you and your leadership training are welcome here in Sri Lanka. If you host your training in a nice Colombo (Sri Lanka's capital) hotel with a nice venue and a buffet lunch, we can get fifty to one hundred pastors and ministry leaders to come. They will come, and you can get some great pictures for your newsletter. Then, after the seminar, they will take your manual home with them and put it on the shelf with [U.S. megachurch pastor's] training manual and [another U.S. mega-church pastor's] training manual and [a well-known U.S. leadership trainer's] training manual, and they will go about their own ministry in their own way.

When we reported his response to our organizational president, we all agreed that we were not needed in Sri Lanka. A year later, however, our Sri Lankan friend contacted us and said, "There is something you can help us with." He asked that I draw on my past experience in youth ministry to help them with creating a vision for youth worker training. This was neither our organizational focus nor my most up-to-date area of expertise, but we again agreed that, in order to follow our desire to come alongside our colleagues to help them fulfill their vision, Christie and I would go do youth worker training.

We returned to teach every two years for a decade, and as we did, we grew to understand the Sri Lankan context a little better. In addition, our organization developed newer training materials designed to adjust to specific contexts—that is, not just a "This worked in the United States so we're exporting it to you" type of training. Ten years after our listening trip, this resulted in a joint partnership with a Sri Lankan training institution now providing a master of arts degree in organizational leadership for pastors and ministry leaders.

The bottom line is this: moving ahead together will take time, listening and long-term relational credibility.

So Where Do We Fit in the Global Church?

When I started envisioning this book, I was hoping to provide a neat and tidy answer to that question. I now know I cannot. If you pushed me to answer the question, I'd simply respond, "It depends."

It depends on relationship building, humble attitudes, a learning spirit and acute listening, which are all subjects in the chapters ahead. It depends on the cultural context of the outreach. Fitting with the Egyptian church in an effort to reach out to Iraq differs greatly from joining the Ecuadoran church to reach out to the indigenous Quechua people. Outreach in southern Africa differs greatly from outreach across North Africa.

The Mission Commission of the World Evangelical Alliance, a multicultural gathering of global mission leaders, summarized one of their global consultations this way: "Certain themes emerged: the challenge of developing adequate mission practice in and from contexts of complexity, uncertainty and change; and the reality of multiple approaches to mission and its practice."[3] So how do we understand where we fit? In short: it depends.

Some Things Never Change

In the pursuit to understand global partnerships and mutual missiology, certain truths must be at the foundation for the church, whether in North America or in the Majority World. To establish our foundation, let's open this section by a quick look at the passage referred to earlier as the Great Compassion: Matthew 25:31-46.[4]

Certain verses in the Bible exist to rattle our cages. They explode off the page to wake us up and cause us to reevaluate. Jesus' words about the judgment of the nations and the separation of the sheep from the goats certainly qualify. The Lord awakens his followers to the real definition of the gospel by explaining that God's judgment will be based on how we cared for people in need.

He reminds us that a visit to a prisoner, compassion to the impoverished (the giving of food to the hungry, drink to the thirsty, and clothes to the naked) and a visit to the lonely reflect our true love for him. If we are the people of Christ, we are supposed to be characterized by hospitality to the outcast and outreach to the poor. Omitting these practices results in eternal judgment. This sounds harsh, but it accurately portrays Jesus' concern that our faith touches the disadvantaged.

James puts it more bluntly in his letter designed to remind us that "faith without deeds is dead" (Jas 2:26). "Pure and faultless" religion, James writes, is "to look after orphans and widows in their distress and to keep oneself from being polluted by the world" (Jas 1:27). James wrote to people preoccupied with status (see Jas 2:1-13 on the issue of showing partiality to the rich). In contrast to their natural inclinations, he exhorted them to demonstrate their faith by reaching out to those without status—namely, widows and orphans. Giving to those who cannot give back marks our religion as "pure and faultless."

Jesus and James both endorse the same truth. They tell us that the genuineness of our faith, our outreach and our Christlike love can be evaluated with one question: how does our faith take expression in caring for the poor? The question stirs our guilt and causes us to wrestle with responses like, "But Jesus, what about all these other good things I'm into?" But we're still left with the provoking question, "How does our Christianity demonstrate itself in our outreach to the poor?"

Ron Sider rocked the Christian world over thirty years ago with his book *Rich Christians in an Age of Hunger*. He now challenges Christians to pragmatic ministry to the poor by joining in a covenant he calls the Generous Christian Pledge.[5] He encourages every Christian to undertake a lifestyle mission for the poor. The pledge reads: "I pledge to open my heart to God's call to care as much about the poor as the Bible does. Daily, to pray for the poor, beginning with the Generous Christians Prayer: "Lord Jesus, teach my heart to share your love with the poor." Weekly, to minister, at least one hour, to a poor person: helping, serving, sharing with and mostly, getting to know someone in need. Monthly, to study, at least one book, article, or film about the plight of the poor and hungry and discuss it with others. Yearly, to retreat, for a few hours before the Scriptures, to meditate on this one question: Is caring for the poor as important in my life as it is in the Bible? and to examine my budget and priorities in light of it, asking God what changes He would like me to make in the use of my time, money, and influence."

The cage-rattling statements of Jesus and James demand a response. The Generous Christian Pledge is a great place to start.

Questions and Next Steps

1. Based on what you know and what you have read thus far, how would you answer the question, "Where does our church fit in global mission?"

2. If someone said to you, "The needs are so great here in North America. Maybe we should just stay out of global Christianity and fix our own nations first," how would you respond?

4

Biblical Continuity

With our assessments and observations behind us, we move ahead on our journey into global Christianity. In one respect, the big question is not "Where do we fit?" but "What is God doing?" Joining God in his global eternal mission is our first priority.

As human beings, however, everyone wants to feel included. We want to belong. We want to go where God wants to take us. But where is that?

We start with this phrase *biblical continuity* because our first mission in the world is not to react to current trends. Our first priority is neither to maintain positions of power in the global Christian family nor to abandon our part in God's overall plan. Our first responsibility is to build our foundation for involvement, relationships and partnerships on the truth revealed to us in the Scriptures.

So what do we know for certain about the Bible, especially as it pertains to our topics of missions and outreach? In other words, if we desire to build our involvement in the world on biblical foundations—both the teachings of Jesus and the Bible as a whole—what constitutes that foundation?

A Global Mandate
Some people state or imply that the day of North American involvement in global missions is over. Our world is slipping into a

post-Christian phase, this view suggests: the Majority World church is rising, so let them take on the world. While statements like these always have an element of truth in them, they overlook the biblical commands that Jesus left with his disciples after his resurrection and before he ascended into heaven. The Great Commission affirms three truths concerning God's mission for our local fellowships and for the global church in all places and in all times.

On the go. These commissions remind every Christian that God wants us to be going into all the world. Experts in the Greek language remind us that the command we translate as "go" in Matthew 28:18-20 and Mark 16:15 is actually a participle: "as you are going." In other words, we might not know exactly where God wants us to go, but we know that he expects us to go into a world where people suffer and where many have not yet responded to the message of God's love expressed through Jesus' life, death and resurrection. On Easter night, when the resurrected Jesus says to his followers "As the Father has sent me, I am sending you," he affirms the same truth (Jn 20:21). We don't need to ask if we are sent; Jesus says we are. What we need to ask is *where* and *to whom.*

So that everyone has a chance to respond. The "all nations" phrase of Luke 24:47 and Matthew 28:19 literally means "every ethnic-specific group." God's mission is that people of every ethnicity would have an opportunity to experience his love and respond to his invitation to a life of following Jesus. No one should be left out of the invitation to God's family, whether he is a Gujarati man working alongside us in the hospital lab or she is a Kurdish Muslim in northern Iraq. Mark 16:15 expands it to "all creation," and Luke paints our outreach with concentric circles: begin where you live (your "Jerusalem"), expand to your region (your "Judea"), across cultures locally (your "Samaria") and then to "all nations" or "the ends of the earth" (Lk 24:47 and Acts 1:8).

Assured by Jesus' presence and power. Our responses to the Great Commission of Jesus do not rely on our authority or power. We go out under the authority of the death-conquering risen Lord Jesus Christ (Mt 28:18) with the assurance that he is with us always, wherever we go (Mt 28:20). He dwells in us and sends us out in the power of the Holy Spirit (Lk 24:49; Jn 20:21-23; Acts 1:8). Doug and Jeanine Birdsall served as missionaries in Japan for more than twenty years. Doug then founded a leadership development ministry for Majority World leaders called Asian Access. More recently, as chair of the Lausanne Movement, Doug has traveled the world listening to Majority World and Western church leaders. Concerning the "Where do we fit?" question, he offers this basic reminder of the biblical mandate to work together for God's kingdom purposes: "The Great Commission is for every church in every culture in every generation. There are no exclusions. But . . . every church in every culture and in every generation must determine the way in which they respond to this responsibility—in a way that is appropriate to time and context."[1]

A Flexible Structure

These Great Commission commands stand for the entire church for all time until Jesus returns, but the application and implementation of these commands might differ greatly. For example, the "all nations" mandates remind us of the more than two billion people who still have no viable access to hearing, experiencing or understanding the gospel. How will they be reached? For North American churches, flexible structures may not mean sending people directly from our churches. Instead, we may join in three-way partnerships with our new neighbors—immigrant peoples from those regions—and with churches in other countries that have geographical and cultural proximity to those unreached people.

For Bill and Judy, obedience to the Great Commission means outreach to international students: providing hospitality to them and looking for ways to serve. For Sarah, it means joining forces with the "Not for Sale" movement to help liberate people from human trafficking so that they might experience God's love. For Trevor, it means using his science skills to work for the eradication of malaria in Togo, West Africa. For some Filipina maids, it means following Jesus into Saudi Arabia as domestic servants so that they can share God's love with Saudi families. For Jeff and Judy, it means using computer skills and literacy training to touch the people and the nation of Chad. For Uchenna and Dolapo, it means joining a Nigerian mission agency that enabled them to move to North Africa as community developers.

The common thread is this: God's people, relying on God's power and presence, go out and look for opportunities to share and demonstrate the love of Jesus to all peoples everywhere. At different times in the history of the church, various nations and cultures have arisen as dominant leaders in the global expansion of the church. These nations and cultures have made the mistakes of any dominant culture. In the early church, it was the church in Antioch. Then the Roman church dominated. Later it was the colonial powers of Europe, followed more recently by the church in the United States. Change is in the air. The structures and methods of how the global church undertakes global mission are in great transition. But our commitment to the message of the gospel remains the same.

With a Spirit of Interdependence

Pastor Oscar Muriu of the Nairobi Chapel in Kenya truly illustrates a local ministry with a global mission. He serves as a team leader of a church with a vision for church planting, a ministry that reaches out to both university students and residents of the biggest slums of Nairobi, and he and his wife, Beatrice (an HIV/AIDS advocate), enjoy a global teaching ministry. In many respects, Oscar represents leaders who could stay isolated and simply promote the ministries they had helped nurture. But Oscar's vision is larger than that.

At the Urbana Missions Conference in St. Louis in 2006, Oscar issued the clarion call for interdependence. Following on the teaching of 1 Corinthians 12 and the illustration of the interdependence of our physical bodies, Oscar called the Christian community to work together in a spirit of interdependence. He called us together to grow as the global body of Christ characterized by

- interdependence rather than independence and individualism
- reciprocity, by which all members contribute to the benefit of the others (and all members realize that everyone else has something to offer)
- humility, equality and mutual respect, with a stress on honoring the less significant-seeming parts of the body
- learning and discovery together.

Mary Lederleitner, author of *Cross-Cultural Partnerships,* echoed a similar theme when she wrote to me:

I'm sensing that finally we might be getting to a place that is similar to what Paul talked about in Romans 12 and 1 Corinthians 12. I think the primary issue is not if we are from a specific geographical location, be it North America or Siberia. What matters for any group of people is if they are part of the body of Christ. And, if we are part of his body, we have a profound responsibility to engage the peoples and issues of the world with our hearts, talents and resources. I personally think we are finally getting a small glimpse of what it looks like for the global body of Christ to work together in interdependence with one another.[2]

We all might believe that the time for the North American church to initiate, lead, control, fund and direct everything is over. But will we willingly become interdependent with our global brothers and sisters?

Andrew Walls, a renowned mission historian, sees the global church as an expression of what he calls the "Ephesian moment." Relying on the passage in Ephesians 2:11-22, Walls sees global Christianity as a historically unique expression of the "new humanity" built by Jesus' reconciling work on the cross. Along with this challenge of interdependence, Walls writes: "The Ephesian question at the Ephesian moment is whether or not the church in all its diversity will demonstrate its unity by the interactive participation of all its culture-specific segments, the interactive participation that is to be expected in a functioning body. Will the body of Christ be realized or fractured in this new Ephesian moment?"[3]

Back to Our Biblical Foundation

Biblical continuity is our starting point in this section, so let's return to our biblical understanding of what God's global mission actually is. To keep it simple, consider John 3:16 as an outline of God's unchanging mission in the world.[4]

For God: God is the great initiator of mission. He is the starting point, the pursuer of Adam of Eve in the Garden of Eden. In the person of Jesus, he comes "to seek and to save the lost" (Lk 19:10).

So loved: Love is the motivation for mission. God's first message is not condemnation or accusation but love. Unlike most deities of other world religions, who provoke fear or demand submission, the pursuing God of Christian faith reaches out to us in love.

The world: God's concern and love covers the entire population of the world. The rabbi Nicodemus might have expected to hear "God so loved the Jews" or "God so loved the children of Abraham" when Jesus addressed him in John 3. Instead, Jesus exploded his ethnically defined boundaries of God's love. The whole world—all peoples and nations and tribes and languages—is loved by the God who wants everyone to know and respond to that love.

That he gave: Sacrifice is the foundation of God's mission. For salvation to come, God had to give his Son as the sacrifice for our sins. And if the good news of salvation and the kingdom of God is going to be spread all over the world, we people of God will need to make sacrifices: personally, socially, financially.

His one and only Son: Jesus is the pivot point around which God's mission revolves. Salvation is found in no one else. Jesus is the mediator: the way, the truth and the life. No one comes to God but through him. In our pluralistic world, we want Jesus to be one-among-many options, but the Bible affirms that Jesus alone is the Savior sent by God. *That whoever believes:* The mission of God calls for a response. We understand God's love, receive his forgiveness and choose to follow. *Should not perish:* God's love blends with his judgment, and condemnation is the consequence of disbelief or rejection of Jesus (see Jn 3:17-18 and Jn 3:36). God's mission is not just a happy invitation to a relationship with God, followed by eternal bliss. God's mission includes a warning to flee the wrath that is to come: judgment, condemnation, hell. *But have eternal life:* God's mission is eternally significant for us all. His love, initiative and sacrifice call us into a relationship with him that begins today and lasts forever.

John 3:16 offers a great summary of the biblical foundation on which we can build. It helps to break the parts down because the verse is so common that we seldom meditate on it afresh. If we desire to bring our lives into alignment with the pursuing-loving-global-sacrificing God who saves through Jesus Christ, a John 3:16 worldview is a great place to start.

Questions and Next Steps

1. As you look over these biblical mandates for mission, ask yourself, "Are these mandates evident in the way that I live?"

2. Is your view of mission involvement based on old paradigms and structures? Are you willing to adapt a more flexible view so that God can take you to new places?

3. What gifts do you and your fellowship bring to help the global church fulfill the biblical mandate?

4. How can you and your fellowship develop a spirit of interdependence with global partners?

5

A Posture of Humility

When we read the history of modern missions, from the late eighteenth century to the present, we encounter courageous pioneers, sacrificial Bible translators and diligent servants of Christ who persevered through unimaginable sufferings. As we read on, however, we also come to words like *triumphalism* and *paternalism* and *neocolonialism* and *cultural imperialism*.

Mission history is dotted with stories of faithful servants, but it is also tainted with human error, the abuse of power and expressions of cultural superiority. Christians from Europe and North America pioneered the abolition of slavery, but some of their contemporaries in the early twentieth century were still discussing whether Africans had full souls. Crosscultural missionaries went out to present Christ, but they often were unaware of the cultural and nationalistic biases that they carried with them. Those of us with a Western or European heritage can take pride in the work that missionaries did, which laid the foundation for the global expansion of Christianity in the twentieth and twenty-first centuries. But we feel ashamed of and need to repent from other aspects of our history.

Nevertheless, we see in the overall picture that God is at work in spite of our human failings. Lamin Sanneh, a Christian scholar converted from his Islamic roots in the Gambia, West Africa, now teaches at Yale University. His book *Translating the Message: the Missionary Impact on Culture* offers an answer to the question: Do missionaries destroy indigenous cultures?[1] In spite of the fact that missionaries might have come with mixed motives and even superiority complexes, they translated the Bible into indigenous languages and adapted and contextualized its message to local cultures. Sanneh observes that by translating the Bible into vernacular languages, Christian missionaries actually helped to preserve cultures and languages. According to Sanneh, rather than serving as a tool for Western cultural domination, the translation efforts of European and North American missionaries provoked: (1) *vernacular revitalization*: the preservation of specific cultures by preserving their language; (2) *religious change*: people were attracted to Christianity and a "God who speaks my language" over Islam, which is fundamentally not translatable; and (3) *social transformation*: the dignity associated with God speaking indigenous languages revitalized societies and laid the foundation for the eventual ousting of colonial powers.[2]

God can work in spite of us. As we move ahead, we need to embrace a spirit of humility, both because of past mistakes and because our merciful God can accomplish his mission in spite of the earthen vessels through whom he works.

Expressions of Humility

The word *humility* comes from the Latin root *humus*, meaning "soil." The word humility literally refers to someone who is "close to the ground." What are some practical ways that we from North America can develop humility? How can we move ahead as *reflective practitioners*: thoughtful and self-examining people who are also willing to act?[3]

Tame the assertiveness. Those of us who carry the Western "can-do" spirit, especially those of us from the United States, need to learn how to go into the world to serve rather than to lead. Although I've referred to the positive power of Western optimism, we need to tame it.

A colleague in Nigeria, Isaiah Lawon, knows both African and American cultures because of his travels. He observes that North American culture is very assertive: "Your educational system teaches people to think, be practical and to express themselves. So a child who talks and asserts himself in conversation is actually awarded higher marks than the one who sits quietly. Though I know that this brings a counterculture when Americans come to the field. . . . the assertiveness you are taught in school becomes a curse when you come to work in Africa.[4]

(As a side note: Isaiah was aghast when, in the midst of our correspondence on this topic, he discovered that my wife and I have our own website. He saw it as a blatant expression of our self-assertiveness and individualism, and he was not shy to rebuke me!)

As we, with our natural Western instincts toward initiative and optimism, come to the Great Commission discussion table, what will we do if the indigenous leadership chooses another way? Are we ready to serve and let them lead? If we see our role changing from being leaders to being servants and partners, what will that mean for the way we choose our boards, recruit our missionaries and plan national strategies?

Adele Calhoun, who served with her husband, Doug, in student ministry in Trinidad, observes that humility for the Western church will mean "the North doing what it does in response to the desires, guidelines and initiatives of the South. The North doesn't tell the South or anyone else how to do their mission. We build relationships and listen. We may do 'nothing' but learn and pray and extend friendship."[5]

Even Europeans see the differences between Americans who come with an attitude of assertiveness and those who come to serve. Although not from the Majority World, Cassells Morrell, a pastor and student ministry worker in Ireland, wrote the following about North Americans coming to Ireland: "We have appreciated those who have come to serve rather than sell. It is very easy to sell packages that have worked well in North America, but can cause loads of frustration in other places if the transferable concepts are not clearly thought through. This is especially true of megachurch practices, which are difficult to just transfer to a very different situation."[6] *Listen and learn.* I'll return to this theme in a future chapter, but I need to note here that our Western arrogance can nullify our Christian effectiveness. We need to reaffirm our commitment to humility. We need to listen and learn from

- Christians in Cuba and China, who can teach us much about carrying the cross daily

- Christians in the poorer world about finding our identity in Christ instead of in possessions or accomplishments

- Christians in the Middle East and North Africa, who know something about staying faithful under the pressure of Islam

- Christians in the Philippines, India, Nigeria, Brazil, Korea and other places, who are learning afresh the joy of sending out missionaries to places where Christ is not yet named

- people outside of our own ethnicity who live in our midst, so that they can teach us what it means to have the dividing walls broken down and become one new creation in Christ (Eph 2:14-21)

European mission mobilizer Richard Tiplady writes:

To be effective in world mission, North Americans need to "learn" a lot more. The average American (forgive me) is amazingly ignorant of world politics, non-Christian religions, culture outside their own continent and even world geography. You have your media and education system largely to blame for that. (We've all met the tourist who cancels a trip to Paris because there's a war going on in Bosnia! Or the person who thought turban-wearing men from the Punjab were Muslims.) With the rise in short-term mission from America, we need to see a rise in "pre-visit" learning and appreciation of non-North American cultures.[7]

Genuine servanthood. Too often, we who go to serve on crosscultural short-term missions practice self-congratulatory servanthood. We live in the hut, eat the local food, endure the heat and use the squat toilet, all the time quietly congratulating ourselves on our willingness to serve.

The irony is this: I might be feeling proud as I "sacrifice" my North American comforts to be with my Majority World family, but they don't necessarily see me as a servant. They welcome me as a guest, but to them, I am just living the way they do all day every day, fifty-two weeks a year. I am not acting as a servant; I am simply a new member of their family.

True servanthood is serving people in a way that *they* interpret as servanthood. When Jesus rose to wash his disciples' feet in John 13, he didn't need to tell them he was being a servant. In their culture, they knew exactly what he was doing.

Although written for a general audience, Duane Elmer's *Cross-Cultural Servanthood* has maximum usefulness in training for short-term mission teams.[8] The exhortation to serve others in a way that *they* interpret as servanthood runs throughout the book. The challenge for short-termers is to discover and observe genuine local expressions of servanthood and then to do them.[9]

Humble Forward Progress

One of the themes that I advocate throughout this book is that mission in a globalized world requires that North Americans listen to the advice, feedback and training of our non-Western colleagues. Hear these words from Bishop Hwa Yung of Malaysia, as he addresses the past mistakes of Western missions but then urges our renewed participation:

> The very fact of Western guilt [over past mistakes made in mission activity] may be one of the supreme evidences for the enduring validity of the gospel in the post-Christian West. For

it shows that the gospel has the power to shape the conscience of a culture, even when its propositional claims have been forgotten or largely rejected by that culture. Seemingly, despite being abandoned by many Westerners, the gospel continues to simmer in an unquenchable manner in a society that once acknowledged Christ.

What do we conclude from this? That yes, Western guilt should lead to repentance for presumptuous, insensitive, ethnocentric, and triumphalistic missions. The wrong conclusion, however, is to suggest that we must forgo Western missions because such missions have lost integrity. The very guilt that troubles the Western conscience over past failures points to the moral power and enduring validity of the gospel. Without this burden of guilt, which the Spirit imparts, this world would be far more cruel, heartless, unjust, and oppressive than it is. Only when our hearts and our cultures have responded to the call of Christ and experienced the work of the Spirit can such a conscience develop on the sort of scale that we find in the West.

Thus, the Western guilt complex properly understood is also a profound call to humble confidence and boldness in mission.[10]

Humility: A Footnote or a Headliner?

A friend called me with some exciting news. He wanted me to know that I was cited in Rick Warren's *The Purpose Driven Life*, which at the time was on the top of a *New York Times* bestseller list. I pretended to act suave and unaffected. After his call, however, I immediately went looking for my copy of the book. I dug and dug through the book and couldn't find anything, so I called my friend back.

He told me to look at a certain page. I found the page, and he said, "Do you see the first footnote?" I found the tiny "1" buried in the text. "Now look at the back," my friend said. So I flipped to the endnotes. Sure enough, there I was, listed in the endnotes in font so small I could hardly read it. I was glad to discover it and to think that something I had said had influenced someone else, someone who was now influencing millions of others. But I was only a tiny footnote. A few days later, I read Acts 9 and the account of the conversion of Saul of Tarsus. After the dramatic, blinding encounter with Jesus, God sends a nondescript fellow named Ananias to visit Saul, pray with him and prophesy. Ananias is the first human agent to influence Saul's conversion and healing.

We know little else about Ananias except his obedient gesture toward Saul. But we do know something about Saul of Tarsus. He goes on to become Paul the apostle, the greatest missionary of the New Testament era. Paul, through his witness and writings, went on to influence all of Christianity. What about Ananias? He was not much more than a footnote.

Ananias's story reminded me that God uses us in the formation of others who might have a far greater impact than we can even dream of. The witness of Tom Phillips became a footnote in the long process of the conversion of Washington power-broker Chuck Colson, who would go on to start Prison Fellowship Ministries and influence the nation with his book *Born Again*. The unknown southern evangelist Mordecai Ham would be the footnote who was instrumental in the conversion of a skinny teenager named William Franklin Graham, who would go on to become Billy Graham, twentieth-century evangelist to the world. Susanna Wesley's prayers became a footnote in the global impact of her sons, John and Charles, the founders of the Methodist denomination. The life and death of Betty Stam became a footnote in the formative growth of Elizabeth Howard, who would marry Jim Elliot, write the story of the martyrdom of Jim and four others and affect the entire missionary world.

My footnote brush with fame in a bestselling book, combined with the account of Ananias in Acts 9, gave me a new prayer for our role in the global purposes of God. "Lord, I pray that you will make us willing to be footnotes in the lives of others. Help us to be content knowing that we may not have a great, global impact but that we can contribute something to the life of someone—especially our non-Western world brothers and sisters—who might. Use our witness, our words and our lives to affect others for your kingdom. Make us footnotes in the story of your kingdom. Amen."

Questions and Next Steps

1. When you think of your nation compared with other countries, especially those in the Majority World, how do you feel?

2. Are there explicit or implicit parts of your national self-image that might make you proud toward others from a poorer or less successful nation?

3. What do you think global humility might look like?

4. Reflect on what Jesus has done in serving us through his incarnation, death and resurrection. Inquire what his actions mean to you as you seek to follow that example in serving others.

LISTEN TO SAGE ADVICE

Rose Dowsett is retired from decades of crosscultural mission work. Her heritage is British, but her ministry involvement now, as an active member of the World Evangelical Alliance's Mission Commission, is global. Concerning this matter of humility, listen to her advice, which she wrote to me in a letter on August 13, 2011.

"The United Kingdom has not had the same financial and political power as the United States in the last decades, but we have the hangover of empire and the memories of being powerful and in charge. I think we both find it hard to express our genuine eagerness to help and to resource world mission and the growing churches of the South without being more dominant than we should be. I think the United States' mission community, by sheer weight of numbers, and because the U.S. churches and missions are so wealthy, probably find it even harder than we do to stand back from power and leadership, and from assuming that some of the ideas and strategies that originate with us are just what the Global South is longing to receive.

"The painful fact is that much of the Global South simply does not want our ideas and strategies, and prefers to work in ways far better suited to their contexts—and we need to learn far more profoundly to serve gladly *under* Southern leadership, even when what we are asked to do doesn't seem to us to be the best way to do things.

"Probably the famous 'can-do' spirit of the U.S.—so amazingly valuable in many ways—makes it especially hard for Americans to be much more patient and adjust to far different ways of doing things. We both—the U.S. and the U.K.—also have a long history of individualism, and of separating evangelism and social action, where the South, with all its diversity, is much more likely to be deeply communal and holistic and to read the whole of Scripture that way.

"Westerners often talk of each person's uniqueness, and the need to find self-fulfillment through finding the exact fit for our gifts; the Bible has far more to say about self-sacrifice and service, and almost nothing about self-fulfillment (though I believe we often find deeper fulfillment than we could have imagined when we give ourselves to service and sacrifice!). Westerners are more likely to be eager to do things speedily; Southerners are mostly much more interested in doing things well, and, in Christian terms, patiently building for depth. I think we are too readily seduced by the worldly and in fact humanist assumption that we can fix everything through our own efforts.

"I think many of the global plans and strategies originate in the U.S. The church is indeed the truest expression of globalization that there should be! But we in the North/West mostly have benefited greatly from globalization when it comes to trade and business, etc., and at the moment our models of global mission work tend to be modeled on multinational corporations. Of course, many in the South simply don't want that. They want to retain their own distinctives, and should do so, and not get swallowed up in a McDonald version of the church. The more they have suffered from globalization, as many in the South have, the more they resent and are suspicious of global plans and initiatives.

"Theologically, there are huge chasms between many American evangelicals and most Europeans: we are not mostly premillennial or dispensational. As you know, that leads to huge differences in eschatology and much other doctrine, and therefore praxis. On the whole, I think Americans find it harder to cope with evangelical pluralism than we do, and easier to split from anyone who doesn't agree with us on some point of doctrine or other.

"I think many Global South leaders have lost patience with us Westerners because we have been too slow to be servants rather than masters, and have not trusted the Holy Spirit at work in younger churches as we should have. So if we won't treat them like true equals, of course they will react by saying we should just go away. My prayer is that we in the North and West will have the humility to confess our worldly sins and abuse of power, and move toward that place where we work shoulder to shoulder with our brothers and sisters wherever they are. The fact is that we need to be missional people, just as those in the South must be, and we can't bow out because we are not welcome. Rather, we need to change the way we serve the global church."

6

Purposeful Reciprocity

As an exercise in listening and learning, I often ask international students or new immigrants to North America about the strangest or stupidest or saddest encounter they have had with North Americans, including people in the church. A student from Malawi told me that his hosts in Maine asked him when he started wearing clothes. He thought they were joking, so he replied, "I bought them at the airport after I went through customs." His host family was horrified—which is when the Malawian student realized that they were serious!

A Peruvian student told me that an American host family told him that he lived off the coast of Ecuador (mistaking the Galapagos Islands for Peru). I've heard of hosts and welcomers mistaking Austria for Australia, asking where in Africa South Africa is located, and assuming that Korea and China are basically the same place.

But the saddest stories are usually about North Americans unwilling to receive from members of the Majority World. An international graduate student related the story of the American family who graciously invited him and his family over to dinner after church three weeks in succession. On the fourth week, the student and his wife wanted to reciprocate and host the American family. When the students invited them, the Americans replied, "Oh, no. You're the ones who need it." For the international students, who hailed from a culture in which hospitality is a priority value, the relationship was over.

A leader from Zimbabwe told a similar story from a different context. A North American pastor came for a visit, but his luggage was lost on the journey, leaving him with only the clothes on his back. When the Zimbabwean host tried to care for the man and buy him clothes, the North American refused. He communicated the basic message that he had come to give, not receive. The relationship struggled from that point on, because the North American was unwilling to let his host care for him.

We need to learn to receive as well as give. Our materialism and our achievement orientation influences us into thinking that *we*, the rich, go to help *you*, the poor, or that *we*, the educated, go to help *you*, the illiterate. We think that the word *resource* means money first and education second. Reciprocity teaches us that our brothers and sisters are rich in many other ways.

Affy Adeleye, specialist in HIV/AIDS ministry for the International Fellowship of Evangelical Students ministry in Africa, writes:

> I appreciate the fact that North Americans are willing to come to my continent, Africa, to serve, in spite of the poor conditions as compared to where they come from. In my opinion, those planning to engage in missions work in Africa need to understand the cultural context and worldview of the locals. Some ideas that work in the Western world may not work well in our context. They need to adjust their perspectives and also learn to receive (new perspective, insight, meagre resources) from non-Westerners. Generally they are accustomed to giving resources to those from the non-Western world and find it very difficult to receive. Sometimes this is perceived as an attitude of superiority complex. We want those from the North American church to partner with us in ways that are mutually benefitting and uplifting; that way we don't think of them as benefactors.[1]

We in North America need to grow in our willingness to be true members in the global family of God rather than thinking that we are the "top down" leaders of the world. Much of this book is designed to encourage us to commit ourselves to being global partners, finding where God is working and joining him rather than leading the charge or controlling the steps for completing the Great Commission. Philip Yancey observes: "As I travel, I have observed a pattern, a strange historical pattern of God 'moving' geographically from the Middle East, to Europe to North America to the developing world. My theory is this: God goes where he's wanted."[2]

Combining this movement of God with the statistical predictions that, according to Philip Jenkins, "by 2050, only about one-fifth of the world's 3.2 billion Christians will be non-Hispanic Whites,"[3] we need to accelerate our commitment to reciprocal relationships simply so that we are not left out of the mainstream action of the Spirit of God.

Being in reciprocal relationship with brothers and sisters will force us to focus first on relationships rather than the creation of global strategies. We will need to listen to the Majority World mission leaders' critique of our obsession with what Samuel Escobar has called "managerial missiology."[4] In the spirit of humility, we need to build our efforts based on biblical concepts of interdependent, give-and-receive community.

From his position as a leader in India missions, Paul Gupta expresses his conviction that for true reciprocal partnerships to work, "*Every partner must bring resources to the table.* If all parties do not bring resources, it is not *partnership;* it is *ownership,* and there will be controlling dynamics from the side of the owner. The Western church must begin to intentionally develop patterns where both partners state their purpose for coming together, the vision they would like to accomplish, and the strategy they would like to employ. Then, together they can determine the total resources they need to accomplish the combined objectives of the partnership, and clearly decide who is bringing what to the table."[5]

The globalization of missions will mean a deeper commitment than ever before to mission efforts that are multicultural in composition and committed to partnering. Partnering will present not only the challenge of multicultural relationships but also the challenge of joining together across a wide range of economic disparity. Ian Douglas states the challenge well:

> We need to consider the economic realities of globalization and the local church. Which local churches are more likely to participate in mission ventures around the world? Is it not true that larger, richer congregations generally have more disposable income to spend beyond themselves than poorer, struggling churches? If this is so, then will the new face of American congregational involvement in the global church be primarily that of white, affluent Christians in a large, rich, suburban parish? Will mission be understood as the haves providing for the have-nots, economically speaking? What are the possibilities for mutuality and interdependence in such unequal relationships?[6]

Working at Reciprocity

Several of the chapters that follow address relational components essential to reciprocity, such as partnership equality and listening to stories. Consider these three ideas as ways to work toward mutual give and take.

Build relationships on the foundation of friendship, not money. As you'll read below, I once oversaw a large global ministries budget. Over the course of years, I learned the hard way that, echoing the challenge of Ian Douglas above, relationships that start with money struggle to develop reciprocity. One party is the donor and therefore carries the expressed or unexpressed accountability question of "How is my money being used?" The other is the recipient and therefore always feels that the "friend" is a shareholder hoping for a report of the return on their investment.

In the past decade, our international relationships have been built much more on mutuality. We start by sharing some sort of ministry together, usually initiated by the Majority World host inviting us in. We share time, hang out, listen to their stories. We ask them to train us on effective communication in their context, and we ask them to identify cultural mistakes that Westerners have made in the past.

Time together builds trust. Our Majority World colleagues believe that we are there to serve, listen and assist as they request. We develop trust that our Majority World family will work with us to help make us effective. As the family relationships develop over time, there might be an involvement of money, but this money goes both ways. We've donated and we've received. We've raised money for our airfares, but we've also been hosted, housed and fed by the local leadership team.[7]

The key issue, as we'll see later under the topic of partnership, is building relational trust as we grow as a family. And just like a family, when one of us needs money, we might ask a brother or sister for help. But even if that brother or sister cannot respond, we're still family!

Let your Majority World family members take care of you. I wanted to call this second point "Be needy," because it has been in the neediest situations that we've learned reciprocal caring in our global relationships. Letting our hosts care for us when we've been sick or in need of transport or simply culturally lost has changed the typical roles of the Westerner and non-Westerner. We become the recipients; they become the givers.

Let them provide your housing. In many of the Majority World cultures, providing hospitality gets short-circuited by our insistence that we stay at the Holiday Inn. Ours is a culture of individualism, and we think that we need our space. Theirs is often a culture of community, to the extent that in one South American country, our hosts told us, "Here, after you close the doors, everything becomes a bed." Every morning we awoke with other people sleeping in the house whom we had never met!

Let them feed you. Eating the local dishes with the larger Christian family communicates, "We want to belong to you." When North Americans insist on eating their own cultural comfort foods, it says, "We don't belong to you." On a teaching assignment of a one-week module in Nigeria, I asked my class to evaluate the class experience. One of the pastors responded, "You have come to us, stayed with us and eaten our food." He made no mention of my teaching! Instead, he saw me as part of the family.

Being intentional in this area often makes those of us from North America nervous because of safety and health issues. We understand. Christie, my wife, is a microbiologist with a specialty in tropical parasitology. But here's what we have learned. First, people all over the world enjoy being healthy, so your hosts will do their very best to keep you healthy. Two, almost anything cooked is okay—even fertilized duck eggs in the Philippines. Third, the advent of bottled water has greatly diminished the greatest causes of intestinal distress. And fourth, if you do get sick, it allows for you to deepen the reciprocal relationship as you depend on your hosts' care, which is the point.

Let go of the controls. Material affluence mixes easily with feelings of power. Our assumption of power then gives us the impression that we always need to be in control. Here is what we have learned over the years of serving and building relationships crossculturally: if you always need to feel in control, don't travel! Partnering in Majority World relationships means joining the world of faith that they live in more than we do, a world often characterized by unpredictable travel, unreliable technology and volatile governments.

Letting go of the controls for us has meant joining our partners in ministry without knowing the daily schedule, without knowing exactly where we are staying, without knowing who will meet us at the airport and without knowing what we will eat. Add to all this the complexity of not knowing local languages, and the feelings of powerlessness expand. One of our slogans is this: "Building crosscultural relationships is easier if we accept the fact that 40 percent of the time we will have no idea what's going on." In these situations, however, our reliance on God and our dependence on our global colleagues increases, creating greater opportunities for us to be on the receiving end of their care.

Letting go of controls also means abiding by the direction of our global partners. We often see the world as a host of individual or organizational problems to be solved, so we look for ways to solve them. In his message at the Urbana Missions Conference in 2006, Pastor Oscar Muriu of Nairobi Chapel openly invited North Americans to join the African church in reciprocal service. But he exhorted us, "Don't come thinking that you are coming to fix Africa. You cannot fix Africa."

Isaiah Lawon from Nigeria echoes a similar caution. He writes, "You Americans are problem-solvers. Every time I come to the U.S., I like to spend a couple hours in the New York underground and at Walmart and driving around your road system! I find solutions to problems that I never thought of! I like to watch your TV advertisements! We in Africa tend to live with our problems. The negative when it comes to North Americans coming to serve in our world is that Americans don't easily live with a problem; they want to solve the problem and move on. Here we tend to live with the problems, and we'd rather not have an outsider come in to fix us."[8]

Letting go of controls finally means vulnerability. Our church began a partnership with a church in Kishinev, Moldova, in 1988. We sent multiple teams to join the church in everything from children's ministry to pastors' conferences to building projects. Whenever our short-term mission teams went, the team leader, whether a pastor or layperson, was invited to preach. The Moldovan church endured what were probably some culturally irrelevant sermons through a translator. But to them, the important thing was honoring our team in relationships.

In the spirit of reciprocity, our church began receiving teams and leaders from the Moldovan church as long ago as 1991. In sharp contrast to the Moldovan pattern—and I say this to my own shame, as I helped shape the relationship—it was many years before a Moldovan pastor preached from our pulpit. We had had interviews that we controlled, but we never gave their leaders—even the pastor—access to preaching from our pulpit until more than twenty years after the partnership had begun. Why?

Perhaps we feared that our people would not understand a sermon through translation. Perhaps there was a theological feeling of superiority that implicitly did not believe that the Moldovans could teach us. But at the foundation was our desire to stay in control of our services and sermons, a control that was apparently more important to us than the relationship with our partner church.

Purposeful Reciprocity or Utilitarian Relationships?

An African leader and I were talking about our various perspectives on the involvement of the United States in several global conflicts.[9] He startled me with this observation: "From most of the world's perspective, the USA doesn't have friends in the world; it has 'interests.'"

He went on to explain that people in Majority World countries often see the United States as very self-serving. If the global issue affects the security of American citizens, we get involved. If supporting one nation over another could expand our influence, we send in troops. If there are large deposits of oil, we have "interests."

I reflected on his political commentary, and then I took it down to the personal level. I started wondering about our friendships in the global mission community. Do we have friends or simply "interests"? Do we reflect the community of faith with sincere, abiding love for each other, which is the way that the world will know that we are Christ's disciples? Or are we no different than the business or government communities, which tend to relate to others only when the relationship advances self-serving ends? Are we participating in short-term missions for the purposes of building reciprocal, kingdom-building relationships across cultures, or are we simply using our international opportunities as ways to foster our own growth?

Almost all short-term mission team members start their reports with the description of "how much I grew." And it's fair to say that stretching the worldview and expanding the faith of our North American short-termers is one of the most tangible results. Ponder this critique, however: an older missionary colleague asked me a question that stings to this day. He asked, "Do you realize that the short-term mission movement is perhaps the first time in Christian mission history that the mission is being done for the benefit of the missionary?"

Utilitarianism fits well with those of us from very task-oriented cultures. People become our means to a desired end. We want to get the task accomplished, the finances raised or the people recruited. We thus run the danger of using people to achieve our goals.

Ironically, we from task-oriented cultures usually go out to serve and evangelize and plant churches in cultures that are much more relational. We come to accomplish our goals. They want to visit because they are so glad we've come. We simply don't have the time (or is it the will?) to build friendships.

Two experiences have heightened my sensitivity to our propensity to use people for our own interests. The first came through the influence of Ajith Fernando of Sri Lanka. Ajith and his peers exemplify true friendship. Some have been teammates together with Youth for Christ for more than twenty years. They have grown up together, raised their families together and gone through a war together.

But the camaraderie extends beyond the utilitarianism that frequently defines North American coworker relationships: "We work together, so we're friends." Some of Ajith's friends have left Youth for Christ, started their own ministries or joined the staffs of other organizations. But the relationships have continued because the basis is friendship, not utility.

When Ajith came to the United States on a furlough, he was so amazed at the American inability to have long-standing friendships that he wrote a book about friendship principles from the book of Proverbs. I don't think the book sold very well, though; no one had time to read it.

A second experience in which I have confronted the reality of utilitarian friendship emerges from the past decade, after I left a position as mission pastor at a relatively large church. When I was in charge of a mission budget that approached a million dollars, I never ate alone or paid for my own meals at conferences. My mailbox and my email inbox were always full. Everybody wanted me on their advisory board, and I received many calls from people anxious to meet me so that they could "share" about what they were doing. Then I resigned. I no longer had the influence or the money. Take away the budget, and my friendship list diminished significantly. Now I raise funds for our ministry. At conferences, I find myself looking for people like the old me with whom I can "share" my ministry.

The reality of our fast-paced world makes friendship a difficult-to-obtain goal. Through the Internet, we may have one thousand "friends" on Facebook but no one to help us in a personal emergency. Large conferences and churches may be great for establishing multiple "high five" relationships, but will any of these people pray for us, love our families, visit us in the hospital and help our spouses after we're dead and gone? When crises strike, the phrase from the television character Kojak gets answered: "Who loves ya, baby?" If our only networks are utilitarian, we will find ourselves sadly alone.

We live in a world of fast-paced movement. In the words of one mission executive, "The mobility of life means always saying goodbye to someone." Obviously, crosscultural ministry and organizational leadership come with their own inherent loneliness. But I fear that we have given up thinking that friendship is even possible.

I remember reading a comment from a psychologist who simply observed, "Half of the therapists in America would be out of business if Americans could learn to have friends." I don't know if his point is statistically accurate, but he pinpoints the epidemic of loneliness in our task-driven, isolationist society.

My appeal is this: work at building a few solid friendships. If everyone on your list will disappear after they cease to offer you something or you cease to offer them something, then you're living in a world made up of utilitarian relationships, not friendships and definitely not true community. Remember: God decreed that it is not good for us to be alone. Cultivate a few deep friendships. Make time to see your friends. Share meals. Remember their birthdays. Visit them on location and simply hang out. Call them for no apparent reason. Make them a priority.

Questions and Next Steps

1. Have you ever been blessed by or cared for or received by a person who was poorer or less educated than you? How did it make you feel?

2. What do you think makes it difficult for the church in North America to receive from the church in the Majority World?

CHANGING DYNAMICS IN GLOBAL RELATIONSHIPS

Thankfully, we are in the midst of this time of global transition together, so we can learn from each other's experiences. As we evaluate what true global relationship-building looks like between North America and the church in the Majority World, listen to three leaders from different walks of North American life as they describe the changes occurring in global relationships.

Consultant Jimmy Lee of Create Possible, writing of his experience preparing for a global leadership summit with the Willow Creek Association, suggests five lessons from the global church. If we are going to have true reciprocity, we need to let our non-Western brothers and sisters teach us (more on this in Chapter 9). Here is how Jimmy summarized his thoughts to the predominantly Western audience likely to read his blogs.[1]

Relationships are important. A pastor from Nairobi, Kenya, was explaining to me the biggest difference between meetings in the West and meetings outside of the West. People from the West tend to be strategic, and they approach meetings with agendas, schedules and lists of follow-up items. Many people outside of the West, who prioritize relationships, first want to know if they can trust us and if we can do good work together. The relational aspect and getting to know each other is so important. In my relationships, I can ask myself this question: how are we building trust with each other, and how are we growing in our relationship as we work together?

Sustainability is the key. I have been so impressed by the desire of global church leaders wanting to learn how to be sustainable. No longer do they want to just rely on finances from the West; they want to learn how to build partnerships with the West that result in long-term sustainability.

It takes everyone to accomplish the mission. When I visit non-Western countries, I often realize they do not have all the resources available here in the West. But they get things done because they involved everyone in a local church or a local ministry. They value the different contributions the body brings and allow each person to exercise her or his own individual skills and gifts. In most North American churches and ministries, that is not always true. We allow a few people to do the bulk of the work, and we place people in positions of influence because of a certain gift or "calling" they possess. Many churches place esteem on workers in full-time ministry, but the church does not recognize the need to give equal emphasis to those who are in the marketplace. We sometimes value men in leadership positions but not women in positions of leadership. I have had to repent of that and learn from my brothers and sisters in the global church. It takes *everyone* to accomplish the mission, and the body is better because of that.

Models are important, but we cannot copy those models. I believe many people are starting to understand this. There exist many models of ministry and many models of development out there. The temptation when we see a model that works is to copy it or try to duplicate it. We cannot all be the next Willow Creek, the next Saddleback or the next Compassion International. What we *can* be is the right church or ministry that learns from these different groups. We can ask ourselves: "How do we learn from the work they have done and apply it to the work we are doing locally in our own country or our own community? What have they learned and failed at where we can learn from? How do we uniquely apply those lessons and help our staff and partners learn from them?"

Faith in God is so important. Am I letting him direct my steps? Westerners (and I include myself here) are such driven people. We rely on statistics, we rely on technology, we rely on news and we rely on our experiences and gifts. But we are not always good at learning to wait on the will of God. I have learned and seen true faith in some of these leaders who are being persecuted and have nothing. They truly understand Paul when he writes; "I consider everything a loss because of the surpassing worth of knowing Christ Jesus my Lord" (Phil 3:8). When I am leading an initiative, I have to admit I really do not do a good job on waiting on him to open those doors. I know where I am going, and I know the end goal. But the journey toward that goal and the process of becoming more faithful and more reliant on our heavenly Father are so important—sometimes even more important than the goal itself.

Mission consultant T. J. Addington cites seven global shifts in how the North American church should look at mission involvement, and most of them pertain to how we relate to each other across cultures.[2] He says that the North American church must move

- from being primarily doers to primarily equippers
- from being in charge to being equal partners
- from ownership and control to "We own nothing, control nothing and count nothing as our own"
- from Western missionaries to global missionaries
- from unhealthy dependencies to indigenous self-sufficiency and the promotion of dignity
- from competition to cooperation (from an emphasis on "my" brand to a focus on "his" brand)
- from agency-based missions to church-agency synergy

Steve Moore is executive director of Missio Nexus, an organization that provides services to over two hundred North American mission agencies. He observes that in these dramatic times of change, we are facing new questions, and new questions demand new answers.[3]

The world has changed:

- from information scarcity to information abundance. It used to be that only the exclusive experts had access to global knowledge. Now everyone does. Establishing relationships across cultures at the local church level may be easier than ever.

- from a closed system to an open system. The result is the deprofessionalizing of global ministry and the ineffectiveness of unilateral decisions. Each situation and every relationship across cultures will have its own unique components.

- from hard power to soft power. Hard power (control of information and resources and the agenda) no longer stands. Soft power means influencing behavior through inviting everyone into the process, engaging the widest audience possible and leading by influence rather than by control.

- from "gathering-based" metrics to "scattering-based" metrics. Gathering-based metrics focus on what you control (how many members, how many attended and how many events). Scattering-based metrics reports on the difference the people are making in their communities: not how many people attended our service, but how many hours of service did our people give away to their communities.

7

Sacrifice—Not Just Generosity

When North American Christians tell me that they or their church is not concerned about or involved in the Majority World church because "the needs are so great here at home," I wonder if the issue is actually local need. Sometimes I wonder whether this phrase represents a protective desire to shield ourselves from sacrificial challenges.

In our culture, which is often preoccupied with creature comforts, consumerism and self-absorption, could this argument be merely a smokescreen for the desire to protect our own way of life? After all, much of the Majority World is poor, suffering, non-Christian and hostile to Christianity in general and Americans in specific. If we get involved, we'll struggle with issues like fear, guilt, releasing control, vulnerability and this chapter's key word: *sacrifice*.

As we enter into greater involvement with our sisters and brothers in the Majority World, we will inevitably be challenged financially. At some point on every one of my short-term mission experiences in Latin America, Asia or Africa, I have been forced to wrestle with the fact that my airline ticket to and from my destination probably cost more than my host pastor made in the past three months or even in the past year.

The response? I obviously start thinking of being more generous, of responding with a financial gift and of appeasing some of my guilt by writing a check. I'm not alone. After a short-term mission trip to a poor barrio in the Dominican Republic, Chicago-based consultant Jimmy Lee of Create Possible reflected: "It is so much easier to just give than to face the reality of poverty. I walked away from our visits that Friday afternoon in the Dominican Republic telling myself that if God were to call me to give/raise $100,000 or live in the impoverished area for a year I would choose giving/raising $100,000. That's just me and may be the same for you as well. Sometimes for us—it's so much easier just to give the money than to face the reality of day-to-day hardship of living in nothing."[1]

As wealthy North Americans—and I use the term *wealthy* relative to the vast majority of the world, not to the lifestyles of *Forbes* magazine's list of billionaires—it is often easier to be financially generous than personally sacrificial. The sacrifices needed for effectiveness might mean greater commitment to an incarnational lifestyle: moving into the barrio and developing long-term rapport so that we can work together toward economic growth for the community. It could mean making the long-term commitment to learning a language, researching another world religion or adjusting to a foreign culture. It often means laying aside our own priorities and asking where we fit in the vision of others. It might even mean laying aside our impulsive desire to send more short-term mission teams.

Our involvement in short-term missions underscores the fact that our affluence is a two-edged sword. On the one hand, we might raise and spend more money on short-term mission airline tickets than the annual budget of our host church; on the other, many in North America cannot grasp the reality of the poorer world without a firsthand visit. There is simply no substitute for going and visiting our Majority World coworkers in the kingdom where they live and serve. Until the Western church can learn what it is like in the rest of the world, it can only be a spectator, not a participant.

Growing in Sacrifice

An old joke describes the difference between sacrifice and generosity. For a chicken to bring eggs to breakfast is generosity; for a pig to bring bacon is sacrifice. Generosity gives out of abundance; sacrifice costs us something.

When billionaires Bill and Melinda Gates set aside more than fifteen billion dollars of their personal wealth to establish the Gates Foundation, they were setting a great example of generosity. When they started traveling to Majority World villages and listening to people, they were beginning to understand sacrifice.

Below I offer three suggestions for how we might go about growing in sacrifice.

Start thinking long-term. Going on a short-term mission trip might be motivated by the spirit of generosity. Becoming a long-term advocate for the concerns you observed or defending the rights of the people you met will take sacrifice. Financial support of non-Western missionaries might involve generosity. Submitting to their leadership on your multicultural team might be a sacrifice. Exposure to global needs and opportunities will challenge us to respond, but most of these responses will require long-term commitments.

In our "instant" society, we want to act now and see results in seconds or minutes or—if we are patient—hours. But days, weeks, years, decades? Do we have what it takes? In our world, long-term sacrifice grows as we get involved. It can progress

- from taking a course or reading a book on world religions, to developing a friendship with a Muslim, Hindu or Buddhist person, to moving to a city in North Africa or South Asia in hopes of being a witness for Christ there

- from becoming an advocate for immigrant rights, to getting involved in the diplomatic corps, to becoming a lawyer at the United Nations dedicated to getting countries to abide by the U.N. Declaration of Human Rights

- from going on a short-term mission trip to reach children in a poor barrio, to supporting a child for forty dollars a month through World Vision or Compassion International, to becoming a social worker dedicated to serving children

- from learning a language, to learning about people who don't have the Bible in their mother tongue, to becoming a linguist who translates the Bible

- from dedicating thirty minutes per day to pray for the nations of the world, to building crosscultural friendships, to going to serve in a multicultural organization

- from studying business at a university, to learning about microfinance, to engaging in business partnerships designed to create jobs for the poorer populations of the world

- from taking a stand for an issue (advocating for free-trade coffee, opposing blood diamonds, opposing the manufacturing of "conflict minerals" for cell phones), to becoming an advocate for the people affected, to becoming an executive with a multinational corporation who brings the Christian value of dignity for the people affected by these issues

You get the point. These are not issues that will be solved by a generous check. These are issues that can take our lifetimes.

Start releasing the American dream. In *The Progress Paradox*, Gregg Easterbrook uses parameters like healthcare, options, living space per person and mobility to conclude that we who live middle-class lives in North America or Europe are living a lifestyle that is, materially speaking, "better than 99 percent of all the people who have ever lived in human history."[2]

He goes on to show the great paradox of our material wealth. As our lives have grown more comfortable, more affluent and filled with more possessions, "depression in the Western nations has increased ten times."[3] Why? Easterbook cites Martin Seligman, past president of the American Psychological Association, who identifies rampant individualism (viewing everything through the "I," which inevitably leads to loneliness) and runaway consumerism (thinking that owning more will make us happy and then being disappointed when it fails to deliver).[4] Like the rich farmer in Luke's parable, excessive individualism and rampant consumerism distracts us from the care of our souls. We enlarge on the outside and shrivel on the inside, and we find ourselves spiritually bankrupt.

If any characteristic of North American society might disqualify us from effective involvement in mission in our globalized world, it is the relentless pursuit of the so-called American dream. (I think it affects Canadians too.) The belief that each successive generation will do better economically than the preceding one leads to exaggerated expectations of life and feelings of entitlement. If my worldview dictates that a happy and successful life is my right, I will run away from the sacrifices needed to be a genuine participant in the global mission of God.[5]

Matthew and Luke refer to this as being "choked." The phrase comes from the parable of the four soils, and it refers to the plant that grows up alongside the weeds and thorns. Jesus says that the weeds and thorns represent the "worries of this life and the deceitfulness of wealth" that grow up alongside the plant and choke the plant; "making it unfruitful" or such that "they do not mature" (Mt 13:22; Lk 8:14). It's worth noting that in the parable, the plant lives. It gives the appearance of a plant. It fools itself and the other plants into thinking that it is a plant. But it is fruitless and immature.

Unless we learn to sacrifice our sense of entitlement and the expectation that our lives ought to get more and more comfortable, we will find ourselves increasingly irrelevant in relating to a poorer world. If Easterbook is right, we will also find our spiritual vitality and our emotional contentment sapped by the desire for more.[6] Revising our expectations according to global realities and downsizing our lifestyles are essential if we desire effective interaction with the Majority World.

Start revising your view on suffering. Have you ever seen a book on evangelistic suffering? I know plenty of "why" books on suffering and some theological treatises on "how God could let this happen," but I cannot recall any books about "how to use your suffering for the sake of the kingdom." Perhaps the book is out there, but it certainly has never become a bestseller!

I began thinking about this recently while I was sitting at the diabetic clinic waiting for my quarterly appointment. As I mentioned earlier, I am a Type 1 diabetic, which requires four blood tests and insulin injections daily. As I waited, I thought about how God has used this disease to place me as a witness to all sorts of people I otherwise would never have met: from my Jewish doctor who is fascinated by our missionary travels, to other diabetics struggling with depression as they seek to manage the disease. The disease has even opened doors of relationships internationally. Christie and I sat for dinner with a family in Sri Lanka. As I turned to the side to take my pre-dinner blood test and give myself my corresponding injection, I noticed our hostess staring at me. I explained what I was doing and she responded, "I never knew Americans had any type of suffering." Our friend, who suffered with a chronic disease as well, felt a new bond with us, a "fellowship of suffering" (see Philippians 3:10).

The Bible is full of stories of God taking suffering and using it for his purposes. Joseph's suffering in Egypt as a slave and then a prisoner was ultimately to save the twelve tribes of Israel. Esther endured hardship and risked her life for the preservation of God's people. Daniel and his three friends suffered at the hands of Babylonian and Medo-Persian kings so that they could point these pagans to the one true God. The apostles valued their suffering because it helped them to identify with Jesus and it put them as witnesses before kings and rulers and influential leaders.

Paul wrote to the Corinthians that God comforts us in our afflictions so that we can, in turn, comfort others (2 Cor 1:4). When we encounter hardship, if God doesn't answer our first prayer—and our first prayer is almost always, "God, please take away the pain"—then we can pray: "Okay then, Lord, please use the pain for your purposes. Put me into ministry with others who need to know your comfort." We can pray, "I wish I had a job, but use me this week in the unemployment line"; "I pray for a relief of my loneliness, but use me to reach out to refugees who may be far lonelier than I"; "I'm praying that you will heal this cancer, but if you don't, please use me this week at my chemotherapy treatment."[7]

Jesus provides the ultimate example of evangelistic suffering. Although he wanted to be relieved of the cross ahead of him, he prayed, "Yet not my will, but yours be done" (Lk 22:42). God can take our history of past physical or sexual abuse and use it to enable us to get involved with ministries that rescue people from some form of human trafficking.[8] God can take our past painful experiences of discrimination and enable us to care for ethnic minority people who have suffered in many countries.

Questions and Next Steps

1. Discuss with your small group the difference between generosity and sacrifice.

2. What does it mean to "take up our cross daily"?

3. What sacrifices—specifically downsizing of your lifestyle or your life's expectations—would be difficult for you?

4. What sacrifices do you think will be necessary for you, your fellowship group or your church to cultivate genuine relationships with brothers and sisters from the Majority World church?

5. After this book, consider reading David Platt's *Radical: Taking Back Your Faith from the American Dream* (Colorado Springs: Multnomah, 2010).

8

Partnership Equality

Partnership has become one of the most overused buzzwords in the global Christian mission enterprise. A search on Google for the phrase *partnership in mission* points to over seventeen thousand sites. But the word has many potential meanings. For one, *partnership* can mean, "You send us money, we'll find the Majority World worker for your money to support and then we'll send you results of his or her ministry and a picture for your refrigerator."

For another organization, *partnership* means, "Our church wants to send short-term mission teams to your location." For another, it refers to the array of groups that have joined in *partnership*, which means they have agreed to come under our organizational umbrella or fit into our strategic plan (and we're sending them money).

In his foreword to *Cross-Cultural Partnerships*, Duane Elmer records his experience in Canada of trying to unpack the meaning of the word *partnership* in a conference of Christian workers:

> Five years ago I spoke at a conference in Canada where two-thirds of the attendees were Canadian missionaries and the remaining one-third were First Nations people. The conference theme was "Partnership." After opening remarks, I asked the group a question: "What comes to your mind when you hear

the word *partnership*?" The missionary members offered words like *mutuality, sharing, respect, cooperation, collaboration* and so on. It struck me that, as far as I could tell, none of the First Nations people had spoken. After a long silence, a First Nations person spoke firmly but dispassionately: "When we hear the word *partnership*, what comes to our mind is that this is another way for the White man to control us."[1]

North American mission leaders offer the same basic critique. Joe Handley, president of Asian Access, a ministry dedicated to coming alongside of leaders across Asia, writes:

> Unfortunately, for the most part, the North American mission force talks a great game about partnership, but paternalism and colonial patterns still predominate. My sense is that the global church would love to partner but isn't interested in the strings that are attached or the models of ministry we bring. Rather, they are looking for friends who model Christlike family: servant-oriented to help lift up and encourage / empower. Thus, servant-based friendship that brings resources at the right time and measurements but does so without control. This friendship requires unique listening skills and sensitivity to the cultural milieu and cues in each region.[2]

Richard Tiplady of the European Missionary Association observes, "We have to be very careful about how we use and understand that word *partner*. For many Northern/Western Christians (and I include Europeans here alongside North Americans), our 'partners' are those people in Latin America, Africa or Asia *whom we help*. That's not partnership."[3]

Ron Blue, veteran missionary and an adjunct professor in world missions and intercultural studies at Dallas Theological Seminary, says that although we in North America talk much about *partnership*, in reality we're talking about *sponsorship*. He observes, "It appears to me that those of us in the North American empire are rather slow to yield control to others."[4]

Bill Taylor, former executive director of the World Evangelical Alliance Mission Commission and a peripatetic world traveler, takes the problem deeper. He blames both North American and Majority World leaders for the breakdown: "What does partnership between Global North and Global South look like? A respected veteran cross-cultural servant told me recently: 'At the end of the day, and after forty years of observing it, all the talk is great, but regretfully the selfish desires of our mission leaders from both South and North take over. *Authentic, mutually-respectful, trust-giving partnerships don't just happen. It takes more work and requires a kind of humility that most people are either not really interested in or capable of.* I'm surprised I'm not more cynical than I am."[5]

Robert Morrison (1782-1834), pioneer missionary and Bible translator in Cantonese-speaking China, served twenty-seven years for about a dozen converts. Commenting on the need for a leader to be willing to serve away from the limelight, Morrison wrote, "The great fault, I think, in our mission is that no one likes to be second."[6]

The greatest challenge in building effective partnerships between Westerners and non-Westerners is control. This control issue gets played out around money, goals, policies, reporting mechanisms, theological statements and more. It seems that our inherently sinful condition makes working together difficult, which is one of the reasons that unity of Christians is foundational to global witness (see chapter ten of this book and Jn 17:21, 23).

Which grabs our interests more? Our "small k" kingdoms: the enlargement of our churches, denominations, agencies, personal agendas and sense of global influence? Or are we dedicated to the spread of Christ's "capital K" Kingdom, where we care more about God's reign than our church's influence and more about the growth of the family of God than the expansion of our organization's global footprint?

Chapter four exhorted us to build our involvement in the global Christian movement on biblical foundations. Chapter five set the groundwork for partnerships with the challenge to humility and servanthood. Chapter six reminded us that the image of the multigifted body of Christ is an image of reciprocity and interdependence. And chapter seven advised that global participation might confront us with the challenge of personal sacrifice. So how do we build a greater sense of equality in partnerships between the North American church and the Majority World church?

Bishop Hwa Yung of Malaysia calls us to struggle with the development of partnerships in spite of the human and economic challenges: "In a globalized world, the days of parochial thinking and action in missions are over. The task is far too big for any one group to manage on its own. The way forward has to be one of genuine Christian partnership between Western and non-Western churches, and between the rich and the poor, whether materially or spiritually."[7]

Partnership Paradigm Shifts

In their book *When Helping Hurts: How to Alleviate Poverty Without Hurting the Poor . . . and Yourself*, Steve Corbett and Brian Fikkert challenge the ways that we in North America act out of a paternalistic spirit, like a father to a small child: "We have the resources, and you have the need." We enter into partnerships, but we enter with ourselves as the senior partners and our colleagues from the Majority World serving as the junior partners. Corbett and Fikkert write, "Avoid Paternalism: do not do things for people that they can do for themselves."[8] They go on to explain five ways that we in North America sometimes act paternally.

- Resource paternalism: believing that throwing money at global problems will solve them.

- Spiritual paternalism: believing that since we are materially rich and they are economically poor, we must have the deeper walk with God.

- Knowledge paternalism: believing that we are the teachers and they are the learners.

- Labor paternalism: doing work for people that they could (and should) do for themselves.

- Managerial paternalism: taking charge when things are not moving at a pace that satisfies us.[9]

For effective North American–global partnerships to exist, we need to revise our *paradigms,* or the ways we look at things. Several partnership-related paradigms needing revision stand out.

Revising our relational view of partnerships. Being part of God's global mission means many changes ahead in the way that we relate to each other. True global partnership means being willing to redefine our roles. To add global perspective, North American agency boards will need to become more multicultural, international and non-Western. Local leadership will set strategies, and serving missionaries will look for ways to serve those strategies.

One of the most enjoyable aspects of my global travels is serving as a facilitator for a course titled "Culture, Ethnicity and Diversity." The course addresses the underlying issues of how race, ethnicity and history affect the new global realities of the diverse church. The students call me the professor, but the course inevitably raises locally specific questions, questions that I have no capacity to address. From their cultural framework, the students expect me to be the expert, but I see myself as partnering with them to discover their own answers. My job is to ask questions in an effort to draw the students out in answering their own questions as applicable to their local contexts in Africa, Asia or Latin America.

In a class in Burundi, we were talking about forgiveness in a country where more than 300,000 people died in the genocide of 1993–1994. The question arose, "How do we forgive people who chopped our family members to death?" From my comfy life in the suburbs of Boston, any answer I gave would be purely theoretical, so

I started asking questions. Eventually one of the quieter students, Alfred, spoke up. He shared his amazing journey toward forgiveness of the people who had killed his mother, father and five siblings.

In a relational view of partnerships, I don't need to have all the answers, all the money or all the ideas. We come together as family to chart the way forward. We need each other, as Andrew Walls suggests: "Crossing cultural frontiers constantly brings Christ into contact with new areas of human thought and experience. All of these, converted, become part of the functioning body of Christ. The full stature of Christ depends on all of them together."[10]

Revising our economic view of partnerships. What is the best way to utilize our financial resources? Should we just start sending money to support indigenous workers? If we do that, will the Western church implicitly affirm an already pervasive materialism that believes that God wants our money more than he wants our lives? Will Western generosity continue when our resources go to support national leaders only and not our own flesh and blood?

Managing the relational imbalances created by economic inequalities is extremely complex.[11] On the one hand, Christian resources are not evenly distributed. Christians of the Global South represent 70 percent of all Christians but receive only about 17 percent of all money earned by Christians. This puts them at a disadvantage in many areas including health, education, communications and overall quality of life.[12] As a result, the North American church has a profound stewardship responsibility along the biblical lines: "From everyone who has been given much, much will be demanded" (Lk 12:48).

On the other hand, the introduction of money often skews any hope of partnership equality. Non-Westerners often feel compelled to create structures and report results using parameters assigned to them by donors. Westerners feel that they need to hold recipients accountable for the money donated.

The ideal solution, as I mentioned in chapter six, is to build relationships before any money is exchanged. Because this is not always possible, both North Americans and Majority World leaders need to strive toward honesty and trust. North Americans need to learn to give without holding controls. Majority World leaders need to understand where the questions from the Western donors are coming from and respond with integrity. *Revising our longevity view of partnerships.* In one conversation, Oscar Muriu of Nairobi Chapel cited the fact that North Americans tend to think of partnerships from a business paradigm. We come together to accomplish a task, build a building or translate the Scripture, but when the project or transaction is completed, the partnership ends. Oscar described the idea of partnership from a more relational culture's perspective: "For us in Africa, we think from a family paradigm. When we come together in partnership, it's a partnership based on relationships (not tasks), and we stay partners for life."

Revising our spiritual view of partnerships. At the core of this issue is the question of servanthood. Are we really willing to enter partnerships as servants? In his predictions about the future of Western missions, Bruce Camp highlights "the dramatic shift from the missionary being over the national church to serving under the national church."[13]

Traveling over the past twenty-five years to more than one hundred countries, I have often asked local leaders, "Where does the church in the West fit in global missions?" Responses have included: "You have the educational resources"; "You are enthusiastic and optimistic"; "We have the people, but you have the money." I suppose I have heard dozens of responses, but I have not yet heard any leader say, "Well, you really set the pace in teaching us how to be servants." We in North America know how to be in control, but do we know how to follow the orders of those who will lead Christendom through this century? We often pray, "O Lord, use me," but how do we respond when we feel used? If Jesus came not to be served but to serve, will we be willing to follow his example?

Questions and Next Steps

1. Why do you think North Americans in general and people from the United States specifically have a difficult time taking the second place or subservient role?

2. Are you a "capital K" Kingdom person (one who places priority on the expansion of God's reign) or a "small k" kingdom person (one who prioritizes agency- and denomination-level objectives)?

9

Listening to Our Non-Western Brothers and Sisters

Christie, my cotraveler over the past three-and-a-half decades, is a wise and thoughtful person. She's quiet, observant and discerning. As such, she has been an amazing source of training for me in the area of crosscultural sensitivity.

She also knows me very well and knows that I like to talk. She observes that sometimes I talk even more when I'm feeling insecure and out of control (which is much of the time in crosscultural situations). To help me be a better listener and observer, she shared a little proverb that I carry with me whenever I travel. She says, "With two eyes and two ears and one mouth, try to observe and listen four times as much as you speak."

Her advice has paid off. I learn much more by staying quiet. I pick up more cultural signals when I am observing than when I am talking. As another sage observed, "When I's talking, I ain't learning nothin' new." Or again: "Even fools are thought wise when they keep silent" (Prov 17:28).

So how do we achieve wisdom as we seek to navigate this great topic of mission in a globalized world? Where do we fit? How do we discover the answers to questions such as, "Does the Global South really want and need crosscultural workers from the North?" "Do we serve them better simply by staying home and sending money?" "Does the introduction of money destroy the possibility of our Majority World colleagues breaking the cycle of dependency or of both parties building lasting friendships?"

The simple answer to these questions is, "Listen." Take the time to hear the perspectives of those in other cultures, and allow these perspectives to shape your thinking about the questions above.

I have frequently asked coworkers from the Majority World, "Where does the North American church fit in world Christianity?" and "What's the role of the North American church in global missions?" Some of the answers that I have stated or implied thus far can be summarized in specific statements.

- We need your optimism and the belief that change is possible.

- Your zeal, assertiveness and willingness to dive in, if they are tempered with wisdom and local relationships, can be very helpful.

- Your cultures in North America have gifts in creativity.

- You enter into situations with the desire to figure out solutions to problems.

- We need to partner together financially.

The Two Best Answers

This chapter will focus on what non-Western leaders are saying to the church in the West in terms of where they see us fitting. These ideas are deeply varied and at times might seem even contradictory (as in "We need your money," versus "Don't send money; it creates a spirit of dependency"). By far the two best overall answers that I have heard multiple times can be summarized as: "It's all about relationships," and "It depends."

It's all about relationships. The very way that I shaped my question—related to "roles" and "fitting" in—demonstrates my

Western cultural inclination to measure everything, even relationships, by positions of power and by tasks accomplished. When I wrote to Zac Niringiye from Uganda with my question, "What is the role of the North American church in global missions?" he graciously rebuked me by observing that my question was "rooted in an understanding and exercise of power and therefore power relations." He called us North Americans to be more like "the two friends on the road to Emmaus. . . . The answer lies in the Scripture. Maybe we need to find opportunities that create space for us to read the Bible together! Reading the Scriptures together says of us that we belong together . . . and that is enough. What we need to seek out are those whom the Lord may want us to travel with following him."[1] Roles and positions for Zac are not the issues. The issue is, "Are we walking together?"

It depends. Again, the presupposition of my question is that there is some sort of one-size-fits-all answer to the question. Global leaders have shared with me some of the conditions on which this question depends.

- *It depends on the religious/political climate of the location.* In some places, the presence of a North American might be an asset. In places hostile to Christians and/or hostile to North Americans, our presence could actually endanger local Christians.[2]

- *It depends on the skills we offer.* Do we have something to offer that cannot be obtained locally? Specialists with some medical, technical, linguistic, educational, business or agricultural skill can bring a unique contribution to a local ministry.

- *It depends on the condition of the church in the location about which we're asking.* Serving the church in resource-rich sections of Africa like parts of Ghana, South Africa or Kenya is much different than serving a fledgling church in an economically challenging area of Niger or a violence-ridden area of the Democratic Republic of Congo.

- *It depends on the willingness of the crosscultural servant to adapt.* Are you willing to learn the language and the culture? Are you willing to abide by our customs? Will you live with us? Or are you hoping to live in Western-style comfort and come to visit only?

- *It depends on the people whom we are coming to serve.* Serving the government-backed Three-Self Church in China is much different than serving the house-church movement.

- *It depends on the country's or region's opinions of North America.* Canadians might be more welcome than people from the United States. Ethnic minority people in Canada or the U.S. might be more welcome than those from Anglo-European descent.

You get the point: it depends.

Listening

Two ears, two eyes and one mouth: remember? Given the growth of the global church and given the change in paradigms from mission moving "from the West to the rest" to "from every nation to every nation," we need to listen. My wife and I have been trying to listen for several decades. In the last few years, we have been asking the "fit" question more specifically, and this research is, in part, reflected below. I've assigned the categories, but I've done my best to give voice to the amazing men and women serving in the Majority World who love us North Americans enough to speak into our lives.

Here is a summary of what I have heard them say.

Be their friends. Andrew Walls relates the story of V. S. Azariah of India, one of the only Majority World delegates at the Edinburgh conference on global mission in 1910. Azariah was asked to address the question that we are wrestling with more than a century later: what does the Majority World want from North American Christians? As he addressed a meeting on cooperation between missionaries and members of the "younger churches" (as Majority World churches were then called), Azariah said, "Through all the ages to come, the Indian church will rise up in gratitude to attest to the heroism and self-denying labors of the missionary body. You have given your goods to feed the poor; you have given your bodies to be burned. We also ask for love. Give us friends."[3]

Robby Muhumuza formerly served with World Vision in East Africa and now is a leadership development consultant in Uganda. He describes what this friendship looks like in Africa:

> What we need in Africa is fellowship/brotherhood from fellow sojourners. People who will take time to know, relate and walk alongside us as brothers and sisters. We want a relationship and sharing about our walk with Christ. This means taking time to visit with us, *listening* rather than speaking, preaching, training or giving money to fix our problems. All the things mentioned above are important and many times necessary, but they should not be offered as quick solutions or quick fixes to our problems and needs. They should be extended after creating a relationship. What is needed is creating time and space for mutual sharing concerning our spiritual journeys and encouraging each other. Many times, I feel that the church in the West feels they have everything to offer and nothing to learn from the South. There are lots of resources and opportunities in the West . . . of all types . . . economic, technological and even spiritual, and the church is many times generous in sharing these and this is good. But there are also some issues, including on the spiritual side. We would like to be given opportunities and space to share and contribute in challenging and encouraging the church in the West in their spiritual growth and dealing with some of their blind spots.[4]

Learn from history. We need to listen to the perspective of Majority World people on their past and to their critique of the foundation we might be responsible for. We always need to learn from our mistakes, as painful as this might be—especially when we thought we were doing something useful.

Soong-Chan Rah exhorts the North American majority (white) church to repent from our individualism, our power paradigms, our racism and our consumerism. Read his book *The Next Evangelism,* and if you (like me) are someone who has white privilege, you might squirm in discomfort, react in anger or weep in repentance.[5] He exhorts us to examine and turn away from cultural assumptions and blind spots. The United States is rapidly becoming multiethnic. We must plant and develop multiethnic and multiracial churches in America. Rah continues, "Racial justice . . . must be the paradigm by which we build multiethnic churches. . . . We must establish churches that honor the breadth of God's image found in a range of cultural expressions."[6]

Rah speaks prophetically. That is, if we don't learn diversity and racial harmony in our own country, how can we go into the world? To aspiring missionaries he writes, "If you are a white Christian wanting to be a missionary in this day and age, and you have never had a nonwhite mentor, then you will not be a missionary. You will be a colonialist. Instead of taking the gospel message into the world, you will take an Americanized version of the gospel."[7]

Learn from their suffering. On a visit to Beijing, China, we went to church with a friend who teaches English and four of her university students. These four young men were all new Christians with lots of energy. As the pastor of the large church preached, I noticed that he was very old and spoke softly. His Mandarin sermon was unintelligible to us, but we observed the young men as they sat captivated by his words.

After the service, we all went out to lunch together, and I asked the four new young Christians, "Your pastor: is he a good preacher?" I was thinking more of his oratory, his stories and his exegesis. The young men all nodded and one of them replied, "Oh yes! He is a very good preacher. He suffered in prison for many years for the gospel."

To them, the quality of the pastor's message was based on the credibility of his life of obedience and the fact that he took up the cross of Christ daily. The technique and content of the sermon was secondary.

Soong-Chan Rah again speaks to this when he urges us to realize that our dominant-culture Christianity in the West is often based on a theology of celebration. The Majority World church (and descendants thereof) can teach us to balance this theology of celebration with a theology of suffering.[8]

Brenda Salter McNeil, a dynamic African American speaker, picks up a similar theme. She points out that African Americans in mission can use their suffering from racism and ethnocentrism to identify with their Majority World family who might be similarly suffering, along the lines of 2 Corinthians 1:4: "[God] comforts us in all our troubles, so that we can comfort those in any trouble with the comfort we ourselves have received from God."

When we engage with people from the Majority World church, many of whose lives are characterized by hardship and suffering, they ask us, not unlike Thomas asked of Jesus, "Show us your scars, and then we'll believe that you understand the same gospel that we've embraced."

Jewel Hyun, a Korean American woman, became engaged in global ministry later in life. She enjoyed meeting with me as she prepared for ministry trips, during which she would speak in other countries at conferences. On one occasion she was preparing for a trip to East Africa, where she would be speaking to women who had suffered displacement as refugees as the result of an ethnic genocide. She was concerned about how she could "connect" with these women who lived in such a different world.

If you just met Jewel, who looks very distinguished, you would never know that her childhood years included fleeing from North Korea and living with her family as refugees. I knew her story, so I responded, "Tell them your own story."

"Why would they want to hear my story?" she replied.

"Because when these women look at you, they will think to themselves, 'This is a nice lady with beautiful clothes and manicured fingernails. She's nice, but she has no idea of the life we've lived.' When you tell them your story, you will be a living representative of hope for them."

Jewel told me later that her story connected her deeply to the women, as they realized that she too had shared in the fellowship of suffering.

At the Cape Town 2010, the Third Lausanne Congress on World Evangelization, the two most powerful testimonies were stories of hope in the face of suffering. A sixty-something-year-old widow told of losing her husband only two months earlier, when he and nine coworkers were murdered in Afghanistan while doing medical work. And eighteen-year-old Pyung Ju Son told her story of escape from North Korea, coming to faith in China with her father and then losing her father as he reentered North Korea to share the gospel. When she testified of her desire to go to share the good news of Jesus back to North Korea, the four thousand delegates rose to give her the only standing ovation of the conference!

Miriam Adeney underscores why we need to learn this theology of suffering if we are hoping to partner with our non-Western brothers and sisters: "Persecution and suffering occurs in Afghanistan, Palestine, Cambodia, Colombia and places in Africa as well as elsewhere. The gospel is not only good news. It threatens established systems and powers. Those systems and powers fight back. . . . More Christians have been killed in the twentieth century than in any previous era. Whole libraries could be filled with stories of suffering. Some are delivered but many are not. They follow the 'suffering Servant' 'who for the joy set before him endured the cross, scorning its shame' (Hebrews 12:2)."[9]

Learn from their perspectives on theology. Philip Jenkins has reminded us that "believing the Bible in the Global South" is deeply affected by the context from which the people read the Bible.[10] In Latin America, about 80 percent of evangelicals are of the charismatic or Pentecostal streams, and their theological perspectives might not be the same as mine.

Within the context of the Majority World, the Bible takes on new meaning. We in our peaceful North American surroundings often forget that sixty-five of the sixty-six books of the Bible were written either from or to a context of uncertainty, political violence, oppression, poverty, exile and military force.

Some who consider themselves academically sophisticated in the West may state or imply their condescending opinions that Christians in the Global South are "primitive" because of their worldviews, which reflect belief in the supernatural. For the Western academic, the stories of the Bible might or might not have happened in history. For the Christian in the non-Western world, the stories of the Bible are happening now!

I encountered my own biases in this respect in a meeting in Addis Ababa, Ethiopia, with ministry leaders from English- and Portuguese-speaking African nations. We got into a discussion of Hebrews 11 (the hall of fame of faith) and the early verses of Hebrews 12. Our discussion centered on the phrase "since we are surrounded by such a great cloud of witnesses" (Heb 12:1). As the discussion progressed, it became evident that my African colleagues were referring to the Old Testament saints and their own deceased ancestors as being literally present with them in some way. The "great cloud of witnesses" was not just a clump of characters from history books or pictures in our memory. They were somehow present in the room, in our lives, now!

I listened through the filter of my Western theological education, and finally I spoke up. I told them that their comments were verging on some sort of "ghost presence" to me. The leader of the meetings and I got into a fairly animated discussion, and we reached no mutual conclusions or solutions. As we dismissed for lunch, the leader walked with me and took my hand, a wonderful expression of African friendship. I'll never forget his words. He said, "Brother Paul, we must have these conversations and disagreements, because *if we do not, we will each find ourselves worshiping our own tribal God.*"

He reminded me that Western theology and non-Western theology must engage in thoughtful, listening conversations. Why? Because we all interpret the Scriptures through our own cultural lenses.

Mark Noll observes, "Once Christianity is rooted in someplace new, the faith itself also takes on something from that new place."[11]

We need to grow together so that we discover more about the character of God. Like Peter with Cornelius in Acts 10, listening will help us to discover a God who "does not show favoritism but accepts from every nation the one who fears him and does what is right" (Acts 10:34-35).

Andrew Walls asserts that this global theologizing will expand all of our understandings of God and the Bible.

> Christian expansion has taken its heartlands away from the West and into the southern continents. The translation of the faith into new cultural contexts, and the new questions that process gives life to will expand and enrich, if we will allow it, our understandings of Christ. Christians everywhere, including those who live in the mammon-worshiping culture of the West, the last great non-Christian culture to arise, are called to the relentless turning of their mental and moral processes toward Christ. In the process and in the fellowship of the body of Christ, we may notice that the tabernacle is now adorned with African gold and its curtains are hung with cloth from Asia and the Pacific and from Central and South America.[12]

Learn from their perspectives on ministry in context. For many of our non-Western brothers and sisters, the North American concept of the separation of church and state is impossible. For many of them, religion crosses every threshold of society: government, education, family, economy and culture. They have much to teach us on holistic Christianity, and they deeply challenge us to wrestle with issues of faith in public discourse.

Pastor Oscar Muriu, speaking at Urbana 2006, affirmed the North American spirit of innovation. He observed that we like to figure out problems and build solutions. But he explained that ministry in the African context was more complex than problems and solutions. He invited us to come, but he exhorted us to learn the context and complexities of Africa. Then he went on to invite us to join him in long-term partnership and ministry to serve Africa and all of its needs. Arnold and Gerri Polk, a couple who have dedicated several decades of service to communities in West Africa as well as Haiti, write that they see a need for North Americans to offer simple life skills. Gerri, who works extensively with the women of the villages, knows firsthand the challenges that these women face. She urges North Americans to "consider working as trainers in things like planning, saving and money management." Arnold adds that "In the rural context, the need might be for workers who can offer training in vocational skills which are necessary in daily life—electrical, plumbing, mechanics, and health and hygiene. In other words, if you come to serve in our context, we may need you to do things that you never considered as 'ministry.'"[13]

Jairus Mutebe writes from Kampala, Uganda:

> The West needs to contextualize the gospel content. That therefore calls upon the North American church to build a bridge with the other cultures before bringing the gospel to them. If it is brought "uncontextualized," it will be rejected. The danger is feeling superior and know-it-all and transplanting the message and model to another culture, which often eventually makes it irrelevant. So the humility and appreciation of the target culture and, from there, transport of the message is crucial. The North American church already has an advantage of acceptance, but this can be lost when there is a lack of sensitivity to the recipients.[14]

When an American comes, he or she is often assumed by Africans to be credible and authoritative. This is part of the advantage Mutebe warns against losing.

In India, Christian workers adapt their ministry to the context of the people they are trying to reach. Miriam Adeney observes that there are three significant streams of Indian culture: Dharmic, Dalit

and Dot-com. Some Christians cultivate and incorporate the best of
Indian *dharma* (teaching and customs): they are wandering holy
men, revering classic Indian literature and culture. The Dalits, considered untouchable, make up about 20 percent of the population
and have the most difficult time. They exist to be used. India has
more poor and illiterate people than any other nation: forty million
are homeless, and 450 million live on less than one dollar per day.
Not having their needs met within Hinduism, huge masses of Dalits
are open to religious alternatives. The Dot-coms are the younger
middle class: 250 million young professionals who now inhabit their
own special world of money, pleasure, status, dating and promo-
tions.[15] Christians in India customize their evangelistic approach to
the specific stream of Indian culture within which they are working.

*Listen to their calls to partner to serve the poor (and resist the urge
to simply send money).* Prabhat Narjinary is involved with a ministry
called Community Health Evangelism (chenetwork.org), a tool for
church planting and strategy to help reach and develop the rural and
slum areas of north and northeast India. He writes:

> My request is that please, before you jump to any financial help:
> kindly concentrate on how you can be part of equipping us
> (non-Western countries or developing countries) so that we can
> be a self-sustaining church. If you have special skillful people
> who can train us about microenterprise or collaborative
> business strategy and some good strategy to make us self-
> dependent, they will be a great help. Please pray for us and plan
> with us—not financially, but for how we can grow holistically.[16]

Miriam Adeney asks, "How can we serve the poor and oppressed?"
Based on her relationships, experiences and research into global
Christianity, she offers these principles:

- Know when to do charity, when to do development and when to
  do advocacy. In the long run, most efforts should focus on long-
  term development.

- Sustainable development is best. Programs are not much good if they are not affordable after the Western money or support is gone.

- Value-added development is best. For example, processing crops into oil and flour brings more income than selling the crops.

- Participatory development is best. This requires spending a lot of time with people and listening to them. They may not want what you want. Poor people need to be asked repeatedly what they think.

- Integrated development is best. To maintain significant improvements, holistic strategies work best.

- Christian development is best. Humans need God and development is not complete until they meet him.[17]

She concludes, "The poor want something better, but it has to make sense to them." One must take the time to listen and understand and adapt to local priorities."[18]

Listen to their advice on general partnership principles. Reuben Ezemadu, a pioneer in Nigerian missions, states that:

> The Global South is rapidly transforming from a "mission field" to "a significant mission force." In the twenty-first century, this is no longer a dream but a stark reality. However, this does not mean that missionaries and missions from the West (Global North) no longer have a role to play in today's global missions needs. Western missions and missionaries still have a stake in global missions for some obvious reasons.[19]

Ezemadu suggests that the Majority World mission movement is looking for partnerships with North Americans in which North Americans "encourage, strengthen, and resource local initiatives in areas where the church is strong and already engaged in missions." In other areas, where the local church might be weaker, Ezemadu suggests that North Americans with appropriate expertise, resources and diplomatic privileges can function in more pioneering ways. In any case, however, he suggests that North Americans' roles be complementary rather than directive.

Learn from their testimonies. In a conversation with a pastor about his upcoming short-term mission trip to Trinidad, I remarked concerning his host, "Doesn't Ashoke have an amazing testimony?" The pastor replied, "I don't know; I guess I've never heard his testimony." His response surprised me. This was going to be his third Trinidad trip, and each time Ashoke had been his host. Why had he not heard the testimony? The U.S. mission team leaders had not asked. One of the greatest growth opportunities for the team was lost: to hear the testimony of a man who came to know Christ out of a cultural Hindu background, who was delivered from alcohol abuse and who was willing to give up a very significant family inheritance in order to follow Jesus.

When we start asking and listening, we enter into a new depth of understanding about our global family. But we need to ask, because our Majority World sisters and brothers will likely not put themselves forward and say, "I imagine you might like to hear my testimony." When we ask and listen, our faith is stretched.

Pastor Menes Abdul Noor has served as a leading evangelical pastor in downtown Cairo for more than sixty years. A conversation with him and his wife opened my mind to new understandings of staying faithful as a Christian minority. His testimony—which includes dreams and visions and appearances of Jesus to Muslims as the preparation for them to hear the gospel—changed the way I pray for Muslims.

We met Bautista several years ago. His amazing testimony of conversion to Christ, after being the shaman for a village of Yanomamo people in southern Venezuela, graphically taught us about the reality of spiritual warfare in the world.[20]

Miriam Adeney tells the story of Gasem. He learned about the Bible from the words on the paper the grocer used to wrap his cheese. Gasem went to the grocer and bought the whole book in which the cheese was being wrapped, page by page.[21]

By inquiring and listening, we've heard more amazing stories like the following.

- Nicholas secretly engaged in a church-planting initiative in Uganda during the tumultuous rule of Idi Amin. His words still echo in our minds: "I would not like to do it again, but there is something that makes your spiritual life more vital when you realize that at any moment you could die for your faith."

- Assefa was imprisoned for his faith in Ethiopia. While he was awaiting death, the prison doors opened in the middle of the night so that he could walk out freely, à la Peter in Acts 12!

- Feyza from Turkey told the story of an angelic appearance in a dream telling her, "It's okay to study the Book [meaning the Bible]." Joining a Bible study was one of several steps to becoming a Christian.

- Ibrahim from Nigeria relayed his story of choosing to follow Jesus, only to be shot three different times by his angry father, an adherent to a radical form of Sharia-law abiding Islam, who wanted to kill him for becoming an infidel. Yet Ibrahim's persevering love for his father eventually won him to Jesus as well.

Listen to their advice on coming as crosscultural servants. Should the North American church continue to send missionaries and Christian businesspeople and teachers and doctors? The overwhelming response of the leaders we met was, "Yes." *But* then they often go on to qualify the character of the workers they want to receive.

Niyi Gbade is a leader in a mission agency in West Africa that sends hundreds of African missionaries out in service. When asked about people from the United States serving with his organization, he remarked, "We'd welcome them, but it seems to us in Africa that most Americans are Americans first, and then Christians second. You read the Bible only through the interpretive lens of your American culture. We don't need Americans; we need followers of

Christ who come to learn, adjust to African cultures and serve."[22]

In a presentation to the missionaries of African Inland Mission, James Magara from Uganda contrasted the work of the missionaries of the colonial era with what he sees as needed now. One major theme from his talk was this: "Come with the attitude that you're here to work yourself out of a job. For this to happen, there must be a willingness to integrate with indigenous people and share not just skills and truths but life as well."[23]

Again from Africa, Oscar Muriu from Nairobi Chapel observes:

The West has designed a model of missions that only works for the West. It depends on a monetary unit that is recognizable internationally; it depends on a strong economy that has a lot of disposable income, so that a lot of missionaries don't even go to the church for support. They go to the general community, to their networks of friends and family. In Kenya, you cannot support yourself that way as a missionary. Likewise, Americans enter the economically depressed communities of the world with a lot of resources. They come and stay in hotels. Paul's model says, "Stay with whomever opens their door to you."

When I come to America, I depend on the goodwill of Christians in this country to open their doors, because I can't afford to stay in hotels. But when Americans come to Kenya, they prefer to stay in the hotels. We are a very hospitable people. But we've found that Americans want their space. They want to be picked up from a hotel in the morning and be dropped back in the evening. And they can afford to pay for their space. They can afford to eat what they want. They can, in a sense, travel with a little bubble of America around them. But the two-thirds world cannot afford this model.[24]

Reuben Ezemadu, whose work with a host of international agencies has given him a broad perspective of missions in the Majority World, observes that if North Americans are going to serve with those in the non-West, they need to come prepared with orientation on what to expect, experience or even suffer in the places of their assignment (Mt 10:9-42). When asked the prime character and spiritual qualities they want to see in North Americans, he responded: "integrity of heart; skillful hand (Ps 72:78); deep personal relationship with God; humility, diligence and respect for others."[25]

Listen to their specific requests. Many Majority World Christians responded with specific ways that they want to partner with the North American church. These seven categories, built on the foundation of relationships and listening, identify what they see as areas where we can work together.

1. *Equipping.* Sam Thomas served as a medical doctor in north India for several decades before dedicating himself to full-time leadership training. He notes that the greatest help North American ministries can offer the church in India is by "building up a few key leaders and partnering with organizations with credibility (not just individuals). . . . If their resources, like material and money and teaching skills, are invested into the lives of a few and can equip them, it will be well spent. The Western church will fit into this supporting role—ensuring accountability—and not a pioneering role to build up their ministries. They should give up the idea of building up their ministries, but meaningfully partner with the global church in strengthening their hands."[26]

Phil Chinn has dedicated his life to helping the church in North America join in genuine partnership with the church in the Majority World, especially the church in the most difficult parts of the world. Based on his experience with the Majority World church, he calls the North American church "to help train and mobilize the indigenous church in areas such as governance, church planting, orality ministry, organizational development and discipleship training."[27] He asserts that the church in North America can also "help the indigenous church by providing holistic ministry projects through the indigenous church. Projects such as supplying fresh water, ministry to women/children, sending medical teams and assisting in famine areas through the indigenous church all serve to display the love of Christ for the people and opens the door to share the good news."[28]

Bobby Bose, who hails from Calcutta, India, and now works in multicultural ministry in Boston, echoes this theme: "Because of the long experience the North American church has, it should not shy away from providing leadership in the global church when they are requested by others to do so, but they should do it in a way that makes others feel as much equal partners and not in an invasive, paternalistic way. Actually, the North American church can play a leading role in nurturing global leaders from other parts of the world just like Jesus did with the disciples, even predicting that they will do greater works than he did."[29]

When Ben Champney went on his first short-term ministry trip to Uganda as a college sophomore, he knew that the primary reason for going was to serve and build relationships. He and his team joined in a campus ministry. He returned a second and third summer to Uganda to do the same.[30] When Ben graduated from college, the leaders at the campus ministry organization asked us, the leaders at Ben's home church, to send Ben as a missionary specifically to help with inductive Bible study training. We said yes, and Ben went for five years—at the invitation of the national student movement and under their authority, to do a specific task which they requested. He equipped a team of others, his job was completed and he came home.

2. Cooperating to reach unreached people groups. In addition to the task of equipping, Bobby Bose adds:

There are still many unreached peoples in the world and the North American Church can play a key role in partnership with many other reached peoples to work together to reach the whole world. To some of these places of unreached peoples, the North American church can send gifted individuals to work with gifted individuals from other parts of the world, but to some other areas, they might serve best by helping with necessary resources so that gifted individuals of the same unreached people groups or nearby reached people group can serve the unreached peoples with minimal cultural learning (compared to North Americans).[31]

3. Mentoring. Eva Lee writes from Hong Kong that one of the great needs in the Majority World is for mentoring. "What many young leaders in China and Asia need is mentoring," she writes. "When they came to know Christ, they were forced to serve right away, without really being nurtured. What is in the head (information) is far from how to live it out. They don't have role models around them. Western churches can identify one place (one location, one minority group, etc.) and start developing long-term friendships and relationships, and continue going there to mentor the local groups.[32]

Although not a representative of the Majority World church, Cassells Morrell of Ireland writes of a positive mentoring example in Ireland.

> One North American agency serving here in Ireland has for quite a number of years sought to mentor and support Irish church planters—meeting up with them regularly for prayer and encouragement and yet not taking over from them. It's slow and unsung work and probably doesn't make a big splash in prayer letters home. But they have demonstrated solid, long-term commitment to seeing the indigenous church grow and develop.[33]

4. Technology. Isaiah Lawon pastors a very mission-oriented church in Ibadan, Nigeria, oversees the leadership of Full Stature Mission International and has served in the leadership of the Nigeria Evangelical Missions Association. When asked about the role of the North American church, one of his top-priority requests was for assistance in technology: "The American church can use her resources to enable the setting up of radio stations in Africa for the broadcast of the gospel. The American church has the technicians, the equipment and the know-how to spread the word of God. They can enable Internet systems to cover the elite in many nations."[34]

5. *Ideas.* Durwood Snead, global outreach pastor at North Point Community Church in Georgia, reports that a colleague from Central Asia asked for "training, resources and ideas." He accurately points out that we in North America

> get the opportunity to work with people all over the world and we see things that work and things that do not and why. We must bring the ideas we see to those who have never seen or experienced them. For example, there are some wonderfully effective strategies among nonliterate learners that can be brought to many other places where people cannot learn or come to Christ through written material since they cannot read, even if the material were in their own language. Other ideas relate to business as a strategy for ministry, effective ways of eliminating poverty, innovative ways of caring for orphans and those in need.[35]

6. *Teaching on giving and generosity.* Jairus Mutebe writes from Kampala, Uganda, that teaching about giving is critical for Majority World churches. "The African church especially needs to be taught to give and not to be 'fleeced,'" he writes. "I think there is a resistance to giving because of local ministers who have abused this discipline. They have sometime copied this habit from others. Proper teaching here is necessary."[36]

7. *Expansion of a global vision.* "Thinking globally" is relatively easy for those of us in North America. We travel easily and access global data at the strike of a key or the upload of an app. Short-term mission involves upward of one million North Americans annually going out and seeing many various cultures in the world.

As we enter the global church, we must remember that part of our global vision stems from our affluence. The Majority World pastor cannot afford a two-week mission trip that costs two thousand dollars; that amount may equal the pastor's annual salary! So one of the challenges we face in North America is helping stir a biblical vision for global mission without wrapping it in the covering of North American power and affluence.

The "Mission Director Track" at InterVarsity's Urbana conferences seeks to expand this vision as leaders from Latin America, Asia and Africa go behind the scenes to learn from the more than sixty years of accumulated skills compiled by InterVarsity in challenging students for global missions. These global leaders are then given full freedom to contextualize and adapt the useful principles (and discard the rest!) as they return home to organize conferences or seminars to bring the world before their students.

Listen to their admonitions as to "where do we go from here?" How might Americans respond to the call to global missions? Bishop Hwa Yung of Malaysia admonishes the North American church in two areas:

First, the American church must recover a renewed confidence in the gospel of Jesus Christ. Paul expressed his conviction clearly in Romans 1:16: "For I am not ashamed of the gospel, because it is the power of God that brings salvation to everyone who believes." Francis Schaeffer, commenting on this passage, said that "salvation has something to say not only to the individual man but also to the culture. . . . It is going to have the answers that men need . . . because it is the power of God unto salvation in every single area; it has answers for both eternity and now."

Second, a renewed confidence must not lead Americans to forget past mistakes. As many have noted, when Americans go overseas, they need to go with a spirit of humility and servanthood. This means being willing to partner with believers from other cultures. Let me hasten to say that cultural imperialism is not solely an American disease, but can also be seen at times among other Western missionaries, Koreans, Nigerians, Singaporeans, and Chinese. But Americans who are rich in education and finances and many types of expertise need to be reminded of this as much as anyone.

The key question is, how can the vast resources of Western Christianity on the one hand, and the vitality and dynamism of non-Western Christianity on the other, become a powerful synergistic whole for world evangelization? As we ponder the possibility that the 21st century may indeed be, in the words of Pope John Paul II, the "great century" for the advance of the gospel, this may well be the most important and urgent issue on the global missions agenda today.[37]

A Final Word: Don't Forget Us

Jose, my translator at a young adult conference in Cuba, saw me off at the airport, and he said simply, "Please don't forget us." Perhaps hosting dozens of North Americans had taught him about our short attention spans and our propensity to forget the people we have served with in other lands.

Along these lines, Gary Haugen, the founder of International Justice Mission, writes in *Good News About Injustice* about the lack of "object permanence" in children.[38] Child psychologists have discovered that infants do not have the ability to understand that something exists when they don't see it. Dangle it in front of them, and it exists; take it away, and it ceases to exist. There is no sense of object permanence.

Haugen goes on to say that an infant's response to objects parallels the way that many of us respond to human need. Dangle the news report about an earthquake in Central America before us and we sit transfixed, our mouths and checkbooks open. Change the channel and, in our minds, the earthquake and its victims cease to exist.

That's why Haugen advocates what he calls "compassion permanence": the ability to stay focused on the specific needs of others and to work until we make a difference. For Haugen and International Justice Mission, this means advocating for the freedom of children held in bonded labor or in houses of prostitution. For the folks at Habitat for Humanity, it means trying to elevate the economic status of the poor by making affordable housing available. For a guy at our church, compassion permanence has been outreach at a local prison almost every Wednesday night for the past thirty years!

Compassion permanence is distinguished by two words. *Compassion* means coming alongside of people in pain, in an effort to serve or empathize or relieve the suffering. *Permanence* implies duration; we stick with this ministry even after the need is no longer publicized and long after our tearful emotions have worn off.

After a service project to the African nation of Zambia, we knew that it would be easy for our team members to come home and put the images of poverty that they had seen behind them. A month after our return, we sent each team member a picture of one of the village children we had met, a young boy who suffered from the long-term effects of malnutrition. The only caption: "Don't forget."

Compassion permanence can involve acts of mercy, verbal outreach to people suffering from hopelessness, financial response to crises or diligent, concerted prayer. It means long-term relationships and cooperative efforts toward long-term solutions: development rather than just relief. Compassion permanence stands in marked contrast to our short-attention-span, sound-bite world. It is love demonstrated over the long term to our global family members. Don't forget!

Questions and Next Steps

1. Who can you start a relationship with from the Majority World?

2. What is your first question to that person?

10

United Together—So That the World Might Know

Attend a conference related to missions or the call into global crosscultural outreach, and you're likely to hear references to common biblical texts: the call of Abram in Genesis 12 to be a blessing to all nations; the "here am I, send me!" response of Isaiah (Is 6:8); the compassionate ministry calls of Luke 4 and Matthew 25; Jesus' Great Commission in Matthew 28:18-20; the vision of multicultural worship in Revelation 5:9 and 7:9.

The prayer of Jesus in the garden of Gethsemane in John 17 gets far less attention, but it is perhaps the most important passage related to our theme of the North American church and the Majority World church in global mission. In this intense prayer only hours before his crucifixion, Jesus refers to "the earth" one time and "the world" sixteen times. In John 17:18, Jesus prays, "As you sent me into the world, I have sent them into the world."

Jesus prays for the unity of believers as they are sent: "that all of them may be one, Father, just as you are in me and I am in you. May they also be in us so that the world may believe that you have sent me" (Jn 17:21). He repeats the same theme two verses later: "I in them and you in me—so that they may be brought to complete unity.

Then the world will know that you sent me and have loved them even as you have loved me" (Jn 17:23).

Jesus prays for our unity *so that the world might know*. In some way, the unity of Jesus' followers is a prerequisite for letting the whole world know that God has sent Jesus. The opposite is obvious: when Christians are divided and spend time and money fighting each other or splitting our churches over peripheral matters, the energy and resources that should be used in outreach gets expended in "friendly fire."

In contrast, the picture of Jesus' prayer being foreshadowed appeared in a newsletter reporting on the concluding events of the global consultation of the World Evangelical Alliance Missions Commission in 2011, an event that included over two hundred mission practitioners from forty-two countries. The author writes: "The event ended around the Lord's Table, an enactment of the global missional community gathered by Jesus from every nation, generation by generation, and sent out as the fruit of His sacrifice."[1]

Timothy Tennent of Asbury Theological Seminary foreshadows the challenge of building "a deeper ecumenism" as one of the megatrends that will shape twenty-first century missions: "The simultaneous emergence of post-denominational identity among many, as well as the emergence of thousands of new denominations, requires the forging of new kinds of unity that transcends traditional denominational and confessional identities."[2]

Given Jesus' prayer, the global church and the challenges ahead, how can we build toward intentional crosscultural unity? Although I know of no easy or instant solutions in this regard, I believe that we in North America must take initiative in becoming more intentionally international and intercultural.

Consider four actions: get to know the world, develop multicultural fellowships, view business as kingdom work and get connected to the global church.

Get to Know the World

Take a course in global politics and history. Read a book about world religions, which are often the religions of our newest neighbors in North America. Learn another language. Go on a crosscultural learning experience locally or internationally.

And buy a map! Research and statistics expert Todd Johnson cites "lack of knowledge about geography" as one of the most significant challenges regarding the church's involvement in global Christianity. He reports,

> The National Geographic-Roper Public Affairs 2006 Geographic Literacy Study paints a dismal picture of the geographic knowledge of the most recent graduates of the U.S. education system. After more than three years of combat and nearly 2,400 U.S. military deaths in Iraq, nearly two thirds of Americans aged 18 to 24 still cannot find Iraq on a map. The study found that less than six months after Hurricane Katrina devastated New Orleans and the Gulf Coast, 33 percent could not point out Louisiana on a U.S. map. Taken together, these results suggest that young people in the United States . . . are unprepared for an increasingly global future.[3]

Develop Multicultural Fellowships

Read about the heavenly worship described in Revelation 5:9 or 7:9, and it's easy to get excited about the multicultural family of God worshiping in a vast array of cultural, ethnic and linguistic diversity. A trip to most churches, however, on any given Sunday morning provokes the question: "Why do so many of our church services look so little like the congregation John describes?"

"Homogeneous units" may accurately describe our congregational groupings. We instinctively prefer to be with people who are "just like us" in culture and appearance. But is this what God wants? Did Jesus die to "destroy the barrier, the dividing wall of hostility" and create "one new humanity" out of diverse peoples so that we still stay separated from each other on this side of heaven (Eph 2:14-15)? The Great Commission mandates, in the Gospels and Acts, send Christ's followers outward to all the diverse peoples on earth. This global mission, however, must be read in the context of Jesus' prayer for unity in diversity in John 17.

Is this prayer for united diversity only referring to theological unity? Does it urge only a sort of evangelical ecumenism for the purposes of fulfilling the Great Commission? The church in Acts demonstrates the answer. While that early church illustrates a unity in the essential doctrines related to salvation (and diversity in the nonessentials), it also illustrates a racial and ethnic unity. The early church expanded outward across historical and ethnic barriers, to Samaritans, Africans and other Gentiles.

Antioch, the greatest sending church in the book of Acts, started with people who preached across ethnic lines (Acts 11:19-20). As a result, the Antioch church was healthy, outward-looking and committed to taking the gospel to all peoples from its outset. It featured a multicultural, diverse leadership team that included a Cypriot, a Cyrenian (from modern-day Libya), an African and others from various strata of society (Acts 13:1-3). A diverse church with diverse leadership became the preeminent missionary-sending church in the book of Acts. The Antioch fellowship became the church that sent the crosscultural missionary team of Barnabas and Saul, who launched the church into the Gentile world.

All of this leads to the challenge to us: have we missed the point that ethnic and racially united diversity are a foundation for mission here and not just a long-term heavenly goal? Is pursuing intentional diversity a challenge for sending churches? If we from the West hope to go to ethnically diverse people in other lands and encourage their racial harmony, will they look at us and say, "How can you, who live in an ecclesiological system that is still dominated by racially divided churches, teach us?"

Tim Dearborn, in *The Local Church in a Global Era,* observes that intentional diversity is one of the greatest challenges facing local congregations. Given the realities of urbanization and immigration, he writes, "The future church will have global credibility only to the extent that it has local diversity."[4] In other words, if we are going to be effective proclaiming Christ across cultures, let's start seeing Revelation 7:9 now!

Miriam Adeney echoes the same call: "Our music and our worship must be multicultural, not simply because our society is multicultural, but because the future from which God is calling us is multicultural. . . . Not just so that those from other cultures may feel at home among us but also so that we may feel at home in God's future."[5]

What might this look like in practical terms? It could start with crosscultural partnerships across town or participation in worship events or pulpit-sharing with multilingual congregations. Perhaps our services can start offering simultaneous translations of the services into languages representing the larger community. One church initiated an internship program, recruiting ministers-in-training from five different ethnic backgrounds to join their leadership team so that they could learn together how to build a multicultural team. Another invited a pastor from a sister church in Brazil to join their staff for a year, in an effort to learn how to reach out to the local Portuguese-speaking population more effectively. Another church initiated an office complete with legal aides to assist new immigrants in getting their citizenship documentation in order.

The common theme is this: *intentionality.* Without intentional efforts to build our diversity, we will find ourselves in isolated, monocultural churches and fellowship groups.

View Business as Kingdom Work

Imagine a missionary newsletter that stated, "This year we created eighty-five jobs in the name of Christ."[6] Or an annual report that stated, "Praise God. Our programs this year moved three hundred welfare-dependent families into economic self-sufficiency."

One way that Christians can work together in unity is literally by working together in businesses. But first, what is the role of business in extending the kingdom of Christ? Is the only purpose of a "secular" job to earn money that can be given away to church programs, mission organizations or those in professional ministry?

One expanding paradigm, especially in the Majority World, challenges Christians to integrate a kingdom theology into our understanding of the role of business in the redemptive purposes of God. In Nigeria, for example, most missionaries assume that being bivocational comes with the job. Their first prayer request is for a work permit—not just for income, but also for societal influence. In Uganda, the Kampala Evangelical School of Theology trains people to be *biz-missionaries*, combining business and theological training.

A Youth With A Mission consultation on business as mission carried the subtitle "The Power of Business to Disciple Nations." It featured seminars like "Modeling a 'Kingdom Business' as an agent for transformation and discipleship."

In the United States, not everyone has caught the same vision. Although there is now more emphasis on business as mission, a mission newsletter revealed that many are stuck in old dichotomous paradigms, forgetting that the very word *vocation* carries with it the concept that our work is our "calling" from God. The newsletter featured an article advocating retirees to use their business experience in mission service, a wonderful trend in North America. The title, however—"From the Marketplace to Ministry"—carries with it the implication that ministry and the marketplace are separate.

Perhaps we need to take our cues from our brothers and sisters in other parts of the world. One organization working in Central and Eastern Europe calls itself Integra. The name derives from a commitment to produce leaders who are integrating their faith and character and business in an effort to serve as salt and light in the world. They pursue the role of business in bringing the *shalom* of God into impoverished communities and to economically disadvantaged people.

On a visit to Timosoara, Romania, I met several of the Christian businesspeople involved in Integra. They stated clearly their integrated views of their Christian faith and their business. Willi and his brothers operate a bakery business that employs seventy others. We asked Willi, "Why are you in this?" His answer struck me because of its obvious lack of reference to making money. He said, "First, to help my family; then to help my friends; then to help my church; then to help my community." It's not that making a profit is unimportant to Willi; his bakery has secured 80 percent of the bakery business in his region because of the quality of their product and the honesty in their work. It's just that helping people is the higher priority.

We asked Daniel, who owns a print shop that employs seventeen others and is expanding, how he saw his role as a Christian businessperson. He explained that his Christian commitment meant that others were watching his life closely and that honesty and integrity could witness to the reality of Christ. Commenting on the larger impact of a company led with Christian values, he said, "Business can heal the community."

In Oradea, Romania, HIRO (Help Integra ROmania) is a microenterprise development program that helps clients—mostly women, often women at risk—start small businesses. The women get trained in Christian business principles, start small businesses—such as selling clothing or shoes at kiosks at an open-air market—and grow toward economic self-sufficiency.

In a country like Romania, once considered a nonfunctioning economy, societal healing in the name of Christ includes job creation and stable, honest work.

Integra exemplifies a Christian endeavor dedicated to bringing healing—through microenterprise development programs, small to medium enterprise development and through anticorruption training dedicated to helping Christians in societies steeped in bribery and unethical practices.[7]

After the trip, I wrote to several U.S. friends to affirm their ongoing involvement in this organization. Jim Willey, a U.S. board member and successful business entrepreneur, explained his motivation for staying involved with Integra: "Christ has been telling us for two thousand years to 'feed my poor.' I've always thought he had more than soup kitchens in mind." United—working together—so that the world might know that God sent Jesus.

Get Connected to the Global Church

Although the ultimate goal in connecting with the global church is to develop relationships and kingdom-building partnerships, the journey into these relationships can take many pathways. These twenty-five ideas and resources are connecting points through which we can start "meeting," listening to and cooperating with our global sisters and brothers who are similarly involved in the work of God in the world.

Getting started: Some basic research. Even before we launch into connecting and networking to develop global relationships, we need some basic crosscultural understanding. Zeal, enthusiasm and initiative are typical North American characteristics. Preparing ourselves for cultural sensitivity will help us tone down the assertiveness and diminish our cultural gaffes.

1. Read a book on cultural understanding and servanthood. Duane Elmer's *Cross-Cultural Servanthood* or David Livermore's *Serving with Eyes Wide Open* might be good starters. *What Does It Mean to be Global?* by Rana DiOrio is not from an explicitly Christian perspective, but it is a very entertaining book for children (and adults!) on becoming global citizens.

2. Before you start sending any money, read some books like *When Helping Hurts* (Brian Fikkert et al.), Glenn Schwartz's *When Charity Destroys Dignity*, Mary Leiderleitner's *Cross-Cultural Partnerships*, John Rowell's *To Give or Not to Give* and Bob Lupton's *Toxic Charity*.

Global networks. These groups and their websites are great sources for listening to and potentially connecting with Majority World leaders through their articles and reports. They also provide links to news updates and opportunities to serve.

3. The Lausanne Movement (www.lausanne.org) is the foundation of one of the largest global Christian networks, at least among those who call themselves "evangelical" or "Pentecostal." The corresponding Lausanne Conversation allows global Christians to interact online with each other related to ideas, movements and strategies.

4. The World Evangelical Alliance is the largest global evangelical body with a network of churches in 129 nations and an alliance of 100 international organizations representing over 600 million Christians worldwide. It representatively speaks as a trusted voice on behalf of global evangelicalism, connects diverse evangelical church networks and ministries for effective collaborative action, and actively equips their needs with valuable resources to optimize their impact.

5. Linking Global Voices (www.LinkingGlobalVoices.com) and the Global Great Commission Network (www.tokyo2010.org) connect you to Christian movements worldwide.

6. Global Voices Online (http://globalvoicesonline.org/) provides a wide variety of international news perspectives.

7. Your church's denominational affiliation—such as the Southern Baptists, Christian and Missionary Alliance, Evangelical Free Church and many others—can connect you to global mission conversations.

8. Organizations that connect the North American church, its people and resources to the non-Western church include those in the Coalition on the Support of Indigenous Ministries (COSIM) network (www.cosim.info), such as Partners International (www

.partnersintl.org). COSIM also has an annual conference.

9. The International Fellowship of Evangelical Students (www
.ifesworld.org) can introduce you to a global network of ministries to university students. Choose a country and start praying, and then inquire about leaders and students with whom you might correspond. Who knows where the friendships might go?

10. Youth for Christ International (www.yfci.org) includes networks related to ministry to adolescents worldwide.

11. Youth With A Mission (www.ywam.org) has been a pioneer in mobilizing people from every nation to every nation. They have a presence in most countries of the world.

12. Operation Mobilisation (www.om.org) specializes in releasing local believers for ministry; there are Operation Mobilisation entities in more than forty countries, with the largest being in India.

Global research centers. These centers are sources of global statistics and places where global leaders come to study; they can link you to movements and, ultimately, to people.

13. Operation World (www.operationworld.org) offers country-by-country data for information and prayer.

14. Center for the Study of Global Christianity at Gordon-Conwell Theological Seminary (www.gordonconwell.edu/resources/Center-for-the-Study-of-Global-Christianity.cfm) does extensive global research and offers a host of online and print resources.

15. Overseas Ministries Study Center (www.omsc.org) in New Haven, Connecticut, offers seminars and one-week intensives primarily led by Majority World scholars and leaders.

Global mission conferences. Global mission conferences (many of which are related to the global networks cited above) provide opportunity to hear speakers and seminar leaders from around the world as well as open the doors for initial face-to-face meetings.

16. Go to mission conferences where international leaders meet. The triennial Urbana Missions Conference (www.urbana.org) is one of the best.

Regional mobilization movements. These networks can connect you to national networks, regional initiatives and local leaders.

17. Latin America: Cooperacion Misionera Iberoamericana (COMIBAM, www.comibam.org) arose out a conference in Brazil in 1987 where leaders of Spanish and Portuguese speakers in Latin America declared that they were committed to being a mission force rather than a mission field.

18. Middle East: Arab World Evangelical Ministers' Association (AWEMA, www.awema.org) provides encouragement and resources for Christian leaders in the Arabic-speaking world.

19. Africa: Movement for African National Initiatives (MANI, www.maniafrica.com) is a continent-wide movement designed to get African leaders working together to form new missions initiatives from the African continent to the world. The Association of Evangelicals in Africa (www.aeafrica.org) is another resource.

20. Asia: Asia Missions Association (AMA, www.asiamissions.net) works to connect Christian leaders in the continent that represents 60 percent of the world's population and many of the world's unreached peoples. The Asia Evangelical Alliance (www.asiaevangelicals.org) is another resource.

Personal and local ways to get started. Most of us will not go as long-time missionaries serving in crosscultural settings, but all of us can find ways to enlarge our global outreach from our home base. It might mean following up on a short-term mission trip or finding international people in our neighborhoods, but we can expand our influence simply by remembering that *global ministry begins here.*

21. When you come home from a short-term mission trip, think of at

least one person with whom you can stay in touch. Or think through past short-term mission experiences and some of the local Christians you met. Renew correspondence with them.

22. Repeat your short-term mission efforts to the same locale so that the focus moves from tasks accomplished to relationships built.

23. Get involved in providing hospitality to international students.

24. Get involved in local ministry to refugees and, through them, start connecting back to their countries of origin.

25. Look around your nearest big city and discover the immigrant populations and immigrant-focused churches that are nearby. Discover who is already in your midst and the countries from which they have come. Two recommended resources here are M. Daniel Carroll R.'s *Christians at the Border* and Matthew Soerens and Jenny Hwang's *Welcoming the Stranger.*

Questions and Next Steps

1. In the next twenty-four hours, what's the first small step of intentionality that you need to take to start expanding your global vision?

2. Over the next week, what might you read to get you started expanding your current vision for the world?

3. With your small group, can you identify one local effort you can make over the coming month to connect with Christians who are culturally different from you and your group?

Conclusion

Responding to the Invitation

Do you get a sense of the complexities ahead? Navigating the journey that the global church has been called to—with our abundant histories, economics, politics, global challenges and the reality of human frailties—can seem quite overwhelming. How can we say yes to God's invitation to join his global mission? Where do we fit? How does God want us to move ahead?

Three Images

As we say yes to God's global invitation, consider these images of our future together in global missions.

The North American church as passing the baton (or the torch). At some point in the discussion of global leadership in missions, someone frequently states, "the baton has been passed to [Africa, South Korea, Latin America, etc.]." Using the image of a relay race, the comment often carries with it the explanation that Europe led the race in the nineteenth century, the U.S. carried the baton in the twentieth century, and now the twenty-first-century baton belongs to the new senders from the Majority World.

The image helpfully depicts some good changes and the change to Majority World leadership. The image breaks down, however, in this regard: when the leader passes the baton to the next runner, the former leader stops running. Truly implementing this image would mean that the North American church needs to drop out of the race.

The North American church as leader in an ever-growing parade. Others steer clear of the relay race imagery; they change it to that of a global parade, which grows every year as Majority World churches join in global mission involvement. While this image may accurately depict some aspects of mission history, it falls short because it assumes that the North American church is still at the head of the parade, dictating the direction and determining the pace. The image often conveys the impact of North American wealth in keeping us in control, but it falls short of reflecting the transitions in and future of the global church.

The Majority World and North American churches as an interdependent team. By far the image that I prefer is that of an interdependent team. In order to get to God's missional goal, the global church needs to work together, incorporate our respective strengths, accommodate our respective weaknesses and move forward as a family. The North American church needs to recognize how much we need our Majority World sisters and brothers. The Majority World church needs to find space for incorporating North Americans so that we can pursue God's future together. We need to struggle with each other and push each other, just like any growing family. This image of the interdependent team is perhaps the best reflection of the biblical image of the "body" that Paul describes in 1 Corinthians 12. We need each other.

Paul R. Gupta, president of the Hindustan Bible Institute and College in India, expresses it this way: "If globalization is to teach us anything, it ought to teach us that we cannot do anything by ourselves. There is a greater empowerment when Christians work together in interdependency. We must learn to bring together our resources, people, information and ideas and unite them in a synergistic environment so that we can become God's most powerful instruments to fulfill the mission of Jesus Christ."[1]

A Foundation of Hope

Lesslie Newbigin, author and former missionary to India, states that "the distinguishing mark of the Christian community is hope." He observes that our world suffocates in hopelessness and turns pessimistic under the banner that says, "No future." In contrast, he asserts that "hope is the oxygen of the soul."[2]

This hope flows from the calm assurance that God is taking us to that great multicultural future foreshadowed in Revelation. Unlike power-based or affluence-based optimism, this is the "hope and a future" in a sovereign God (Jer 29:11). Rather than the hope of the political slogan, which puts our hope in hope—"hope you can believe in"—this is hope based on a person: the almighty God who expresses his love through Jesus Christ.

Through this lens of hope, we move forward into the future and say yes to the invitation of God. In response to the question of hope, Doug Birdsall of the Lausanne Committee on World Evangelization offered three reasons why he is hopeful about the North American church's full participation in the global purposes of God. He says:

- "The North American church has unique gifts to the global church, including greater experience in working in a globalized world, training and resources and lessons from our mistakes."

- "The multicultural nature and direction of North American society means that our churches can be living examples of diversity in the body of Christ, a living example of the 'new humanity' that Jesus came to create."

- "The rising student generation has the zeal and passion for the glory of God, which will launch them into the nations."[3]

Concerning this next generation, Tom Lin, vice president of missions for InterVarsity Christian Fellowship/USA, says that he is hopeful about the student generation's involvement in the global church. He cites first the global engagement that students are already experiencing. Millennials are the most diverse generation ever (18 percent Latino,

14 percent African American and 5 percent Asian American). In addition, an estimated 300,000 North American students go overseas to study during their college years. Second, the spirit of "communal collaboration" in students—no more heroic individualism but rather heroic communities that are saying, "Let's do this together"—better equips them for truly interdependent partnerships with the Majority World. Third, he affirmed the student spirit of entrepreneurial action, a spirit that says "Why not?" concerning things like the abolition of human slavery or the reduction of global poverty. This spirit of "Let's take action and do something" can facilitate great positive changes ahead. And finally, Tom Lin observes that this student generation faces global opportunities ahead unlike any other before it.[4]

This hope must be tempered with humility. Birdsall added to his voice of hope this charge to all of us in North America. If we are going to be true contributors to the future global purposes of God, we need to

- renounce our American sense of entitlement and make a renewed commitment to take up the cross daily

- repent from past arrogance

- reflect deeply about the world and the Word

- reposition ourselves with a spirit of humility, serving alongside of and learning with our global family[5]

Living by Biblical Values

Functioning in a multicultural world gets easier if we learn from other churches and cultures that have preceded us on the journey. Some teach us through their poor example, as the migrations of Majority World people have uncovered latent racism and xenophobia.

Others have embraced diversity and show us the way ahead. One such positive lesson for me came from participating with the student movement called Tertiary Students Christian Fellowship (TSCF) in New Zealand. Reflecting the diverse global church, TSCF includes a multicultural staff team (New Zealanders [Kiwis and Maori], Europeans, Asians and North Americans), involves student leaders from a wide diversity of backgrounds (Lao, Chinese, Malaysian, etc.) and reaches out across the diverse cultures of New Zealand's student populations. The four underlying aims of TSCF serve as a great foundation for any Christian desirous of effective participation in the global community of faith.

- *True witness.* Before moving out globally, we must be witnesses to the reality of Christ where we live, work, study and play. Caring for our neighbors precedes caring for the nations. Outreach starts with local relationships with the people who can see our lives as well as hear our witness. And even crosscultural witness starts with the crosscultural people in our immediate sphere of influence.

- *An undivided life.* Integrity—living out the faith we profess to believe—must be at the core of our convictions. Living as followers of Christ is a 24/7 proposition and affects the way that we see others, the way that we respond to global issues and the way that we understand the purposes of God for our own lives.

- *Deep thought.* Responding affirmatively to God's global invitation will get us involved in and interacting with complicated issues, like the pros and cons of Christian mission history, the beliefs of other world religions and the movement of the Christian "center" to the Global South. Following Jesus means embracing the challenges of global complexity and thinking carefully through our responses.

- *Global reach.* Local outreach does not cancel out a concern for the world. Each person and every community of believers must learn how to be involved in the world that God loves. From prayer to participation and from friendships to finances, God invites us to join his global mission, and we say yes!

Three Biblical Questions

Another way to examine our responses to God's global invitation is to evaluate our responses to the biblical questions he asks us. Through questions, God communicates his pursuing love: "Where are you?" (Gen 3:9). God communicates his desire to use broken, sinful people for his purposes: "Whom shall I send?" (Is 6:8). Jesus uses questions to invite testimony about him: "Who do you say I am?" (Mt 16:15). Jesus also uses questions to discover heart desires: "What do you want me to do for you?" (Mk 10:36, 51). Consider three questions from the Bible. The answers to these questions will determine how we get involved in God's mission.

What is that in your hand? God's question to Moses addressed Moses' professional security and his identity as a shepherd (Ex 4:2). The question reminds us that we all hold onto something: our profession, our personal security, our defensive self-protection, our Western need to be in control. We need to lay these things down and release them so that God can give them back again to us, redeemed for his purposes.

What do you have in your house? Elisha asked this of the impoverished, desperate widow on the verge of losing her sons to indentured slavery (2 Kings 4:2). The question reminds us that every one of us, no matter how materially or educationally or spiritually poor we might feel, have something in our house of resources. Following the widow's example, we need to see what we have, involve the community and act on faith, believing that God will multiply our limited resources for his purposes.

What do you have in your heart? Although never stated exactly as such, this is the underlying question in the interchange between Jesus and the rich young ruler (see Mt 19:16-23; Lk 18:18-23). The invitation to give everything away, come and follow him was Jesus' way of looking into his heart and asking, "Will you make following me your top priority, or would you prefer to focus on your wealth?" This question underlies all other questions. Will we make Jesus and his purposes our top commitment, or will we let something else rule in our hearts? Our heart for his purposes flows from our heart for him.

A Lifestyle Challenge

Have you ever visited the gloriously beautiful Union Station in Washington, D.C.? It's constructed with buffed marble, polished brass and dazzling lights. It is shiny and inviting and full of great places to eat. Upscale shopping and beautiful artwork draw thousands of tourists each year just to see the train station. Like the amazing airports of Singapore and Dubai, these places of transition for travel have been designed in such a way that you wish you never had to leave.

Imagine that this beautiful train station represents life in North America, especially in the North American church. We invest millions in beautiful buildings for corporate worship. We surround ourselves with excellent music, dynamic speakers and programs for all ages. Life for us Christians is like life in that train station, and we wish we never had to leave.

But just as the train station was designed not to keep us there but to send us out to other destinations, so the way forward is on board the global church train that's leaving the station. The majority of our brothers and sisters live in places which will require travel, tiredness, hardship and discomfort to build together for the future. We are all invited to join the journey on the global church train. Or we can just stay in the shiny station and convince ourselves that comfort is more important than life. The choice is ours.

I'm getting on the train.

A Return to Our Passion

I live in the American suburbs in a beautiful town. Many friends and neighbors hold college degrees, drive nice cars and present themselves as dignified, respectable citizens. I know that behind some doors are relational abuse, alcoholism and despair. But we hold our heads high in the community.

How do I present the love of Christ in this context? I try to fit in. I act dignified, talk intelligently of my faith and warm others to the gospel. If someone asks about our international missionary work, I talk about respectable things like leadership development, well-drilling in poor villages and healthcare for children. People listen and clap politely, but no one gets too excited about the Christ they see in me. They neither act nor react. What am I doing wrong? Examining the example of both Jesus and the apostle Paul as witnesses to God's truth, I discover my problem: I'm simply not crazy enough.

Consider Jesus: he starts his ministry, does some healings, draws some followers and then comes home. His family tries to restrain him because people said, "He is out of his mind" (Mk 3:21). The religious leaders call him demon-possessed, and his own household refuses to believe (Mk 3:22; Jn 7:3-5).

Or look at Paul. He gets his big chance for ministerial influence in the political arena before King Agrippa. But rather than softly introducing the story of God's love, he gets right to the point, declaring the suffering Messiah whom God raised from the dead (Acts 26:23). The listeners quickly observe that Paul, like his master, Jesus, is out of his mind (Acts 26:24). He has truly become a fool for Christ's sake.

When I first decided to follow Jesus, we were in a countercultural era. We followers of Christ happily considered ourselves "Jesus Freaks." To be out of step with society was a good thing. A little weirdness was seen as evidence that our true citizenship is in heaven. I need to return to being radically different than the norm. Maybe my neighbors would take notice if I started welcoming the outcasts of the world into my dignified neighborhood. Maybe I should take my neighbors with me to the poorer world so that they see the countercultural nature of following Christ.

If I were a little wackier for Jesus, at least my neighbors would be forced to have an opinion rather than relegate me in their heads to the category of a "nice, religious person."

A few years ago, we left the job security I had had for twenty-two years simply to seek God and ask what was next. Our friends—even in church—couldn't understand such recklessness. In contrast, a young college student came to us to affirm our choice. She said, "Go crazy for God."

If it was good enough for Jesus and good enough for the apostle Paul, then it is good enough for me.

Acknowledgments & Dedication

Someone asked me how long it took for me to write this book. I responded, "All of my life . . . and I'm still writing it."

What I've written here is indeed the results of a life-long journey. As such, it is difficult to remember and properly give credit to all of the people who contributed influence, experience, knowledge, wisdom and friendship along the way. My parents, Jean and Harry, laid a foundation for a global vision by hosting missionaries in our home. Patient missionaries and local leaders hosted our earliest attempts at serving crossculturally with youth mission teams; their welcome into the Majority World (in spite of all our Americanized cultural insensitivities) shaped my perspective on the essential nature of crosscultural friendships.

Veteran missionaries, local Christian leaders and global leaders have been our teachers over the years. My missions professor Dr. J. Christy Wilson and our pastor Gordon MacDonald inspired vision in my seminary years through their stories and their enthusiasm for God at work in the world. Dr. Timothy Tennent and Dr. Peter Kuzmič, teachers and colleagues, taught me to integrate theology and missiology. Dr. John Stott exemplified what it meant to be a true global ambassador of Christ.

Beyond that, however, the greatest influences have been friends developed through networks, conferences and first-hand visits. Many of these colleagues are cited in this book. I will not mention individuals here but I will acknowledge my indebtedness to my home church, Grace Chapel of Lexington, Massachusetts, for releasing Christie and me in the 1980s and '90s to serve the wider missions community. I am also deeply thankful for the many friends developed and teachers acquired through the World Evangelical Alliance, the Lausanne Movement, the International Fellowship of Evangelical Students, Scripture Union, Youth for Christ and—since 1998—Development Associates International, the organization with which Christie and I serve.

Through all these years of travel and interaction, my companion, cotraveler, and fellow-learner has been my precious wife, Christie. I thank God that we've been on this great adventure of life together, and I gratefully dedicate this book to her.

Further Reading

Adeney, Miriam. *Kingdom Without Borders: The Untold Story of Global Christianity*. Downers Grove, Ill.: InterVarsity Press, 2009.

Bonk, Jonathan, ed. *Between Past and Future: Evangelical Mission Entering the Twenty-First Century*. Pasadena, Calif.: William Carey Library, 2003.

Cox, Harvey. *Fire from Heaven: The Rise of Pentecostal Spirituality and the Reshaping of Religion in the Twenty-First Century*. New York: Addison-Wesley Press, 1995.

Daughrity, Dyron. *The Changing World of Christianity*. New York: Peter Lang, 2010.

Elmer, Duane. *Cross-Cultural Servanthood: Serving the World in Christlike Humility*. Downers Grove, Ill.: InterVarsity Press, 2006.

Escobar, Samuel. *The New Global Mission: The Gospel from Everywhere to Everyone*. Downers Grove, Ill.: InterVarsity Press, 2003.

Greenlee, David, ed. *Global Passion: Marking George Verwer's Contribution to World Missions*. Cumbria, U.K.: Authentic Publishing, 2003.

Guder, Darrell L. *Missional Church: A Vision for the Sending of the Church in North America*. Grand Rapids: Eerdmans, 1998.

Hoang, Bethany H. *Deepening the Soul of Justice*. Urbana Onward series. Downers Grove: InterVarsity Press, 2012.

Hoksbergen, Roland. *Serving God Globally: Finding Your Place in International Development*. Grand Rapids: Baker Academic, 2012.

Huntington, Samuel P. *The Clash of Civilizations and the Remaking of the World Order*. New York: Touchstone, 1996.

Jao, Greg. *Your Mind's Mission*. Urbana Onward series. Downers Grove: InterVarsity Press, 2012.

Jenkins, Philip. *God's Continent: Christianity, Islam, and Europe's Religious Crisis*. New York: Oxford University Press, 2007.

———. *The New Faces of Global Christianity: Believing the Bible in the Global South*. New York: Oxford University Press, 2006.

———. *The Next Christendom: The Coming of Global Christianity*. Third ed. New York: Oxford University Press, 2011.

———Johnstone, Patrick. *The Future of the Global Church: History, Trends, and Possibilities*. Downers Grove, Ill.: InterVarsity Press, 2011.

Lederleitner, Mary T. *Cross-Cultural Partnerships: Navigating the Complexities of Money and Mission*. Downers Grove, Ill.: InterVarsity Press, 2010.

Lin, Tom. *Pursuing God's Call*. Urbana Onward series. Downers Grove, Ill.: InterVarsity Press, 2012.

Noll, Mark A. *The New Shape of World Christianity: How American Experience Reflects Global Faith*. Downers Grove, Ill.: IVP Academic, 2009.

Sanneh, Lamin. *Whose Religion Is Christianity? The Gospel Beyond the West*. Grand Rapids: Eerdmans, 2003.

Stackhouse, Max, Tim Dearborn and Scott Paeth, eds., *The Local Church in a Global Era: Reflections for a New Century*. Grand Rapids: Eerdmans, 2000.

Tennent, Timothy C. *Invitation to World Missions: A Trinitarian Missiology for the Twenty-First Century*. Grand Rapids: Kregel, 2010.

Toyama-Szeto, Nikki A., and Femi B. Adeleye. *Partnering with the Global Church*. Urbana Onward series. Downers Grove, Ill.: InterVarsity Press, 2012.

Van Opstal, Sandra. *The Mission of Worship*. Urbana Onward series. Downers Grove, Ill.: InterVarsity Press, 2012.

Voelkel, Jack, and Mary Anne. *Spiritual Warfare in Mission*. Urbana Onward series. Downers Grove, Ill.: InterVarsity Press, 2012.

Appendix

Letters to the North American Church

In the summer of 2011, I invited many leaders from around the world to share their comments for this book. Their responses have been featured throughout the book. A few of them shared their thoughts by means of letters from the church in the Majority World to the North American church. Below are some of the letters I received.

July 16, 2011

Dear church leaders,

It is wonderful you are interested in and committed to world mission—that is the core of the gospel and the world needs to partner together in this. We need each other—we all have gifts and resources which we should use together. Here are a few points that I hope will help.

Money—is a blessing and a curse! Please partner carefully. It is very damaging when outsiders come in and buy local people. There are carefully thought-through policies that some have worked on, e.g., if you are paying people, find out a local fair rate.

Control—many countries are very sensitive through their experience of colonialism of foreigners coming and controlling, or claiming work that is going on; this destroys many good things.

Attitude—if you come as learners in humility, you will usually be welcomed. That way we can build real partnerships based on respect and find our mutual strengths and weaknesses.

Speed—we know we all want fruit and results, but take time to build relationship first. Also be prepared for the long, hard slog—there may not be quick instant results.

Much of the world is more relationship-focussed than task-focussed—take time.

These are a few observations to help you come, adjust and be beneficial in the kingdom.

Blessings,

Trevor Betts

(Trevor Betts serves as an associate in the World Evangelical Alliance's Missions Commission from his base in Ireland.)

July 21, 2011

Dear North American church,

As I reflect on the accomplishments of your part of the church in the work of global missions, I am so thankful for all that has been achieved in the name of Christ.

Yet, in considering your future work, I believe that things are no longer as they were—and I am concerned that you have perhaps not yet realized the changes that have taken place. I call your attention to two words that were used to describe the believers of the first century. First is the word church itself, which reminds us that we are "called-out ones." I plead with you to stop imitating and blending in with the godless culture that so dominates your part of the world. This has led you to adopt worldly attitudes about your possessions and your responsibilities to reach the world for Christ. Be the church on mission, not the world on a quest for self-fulfillment.

Secondly, I remind you that as *Christians* we are followers of Christ, and thus all members of his household, his family. As members of God's family, we should care for one another. Until we are all "warm and well fed" in the spiritual sense, none of us should rest easy at night. As a parent struggles daily to meet the needs of the children, so should the church in all its locations struggle to meet the needs of the entire family.

I humbly add one additional recommendation. Please send us your adults, and not just your children. I realize that most career missionaries had a short-term experience that played a significant role in determining their future ministry—but I am troubled at the number of children you send our way for one- and two-week trips. Surely even in America there is a limit to how much money will be set aside for global missions, and this must be consuming an inordinately large amount of it. Please send us some people ready to learn our language and our culture, who can then live and work with us to help us educate and develop our church. Related to this—we really don't need construction workers from your region, as we have manual laborers of our own—nor do we need skits and songs in languages we don't understand and music we find interesting but foreign.

I thank you, I love you and am praying for you.

Paul Gentuso

(Paul Gentuso is a former medical missionary to Cote d'Ivoire.)

Note: Bob Blincoe serves with Frontiers, a ministry focused on reaching people in the most challenging places in global missions—people who have never yet heard about Jesus. He wrote two mock letters to himself as fictional representations of real encounters to illustrate the challenges of partnership between North Americans and Majority World Christians. The first portrays a North American mission agency and the requests that come from local Christian movements. The second illustrates the tension that the North American church faces in balancing partnering with local leadership and pioneering ministries with unreached ethnic groups.

July 15, 2011

Dear Reverend Robert A. Blincoe,

In your capacity as a minister of the Presbyterian Church (USA), I want to express my thanks for your church's commitment to a fraternal partnership with the Presbyterian Church of Malawi. As you know, there are more Presbyterians in Malawi than there are in the United States. While we are numerous, we are not your equals in power.

Therefore, we are glad that more than three decades ago you decided to submit your plans to the Presbyterian Church of Malawi and leave it to the Malawi leadership to decide the best use of mission funding and personnel here. As Donald Black wrote more than four decades ago, "the term 'missionary' was changed to 'fraternal worker' as a way to express equality between those serving overseas and those being served." The Presbyterian Church's "mutuality in mission" policy has had its intended effect, to respect the leadership here in Malawi and, I believe, the leadership in your partner churches around the world.

In terms of the task of evangelism in Malawi, the policy as formalized in 1975 is still the basis of our partnership: In response to a referral on "unevangelized people," the Presbyterian Church (USA) says it will strive to recommend new strategies for evangelization that do not violate the principle of "mutuality in mission." They say, "In countries where we work, evangelization and church development is done by established churches and our contributions undergird their efforts."

Sincerely,

x, Moderator, Presbyterian Church of Malawi

Dear Dr. Robert A. Blincoe,

In your capacity as director of Frontiers, I want to thank you for initiating a mission to my people, the Yano of Malawi. Had we waited on the Presbyterian Church of Malawi, I think we would not have heard the good news of Jesus Christ. The leaders of the Presbyterian Church of Malawi are strong Christians, and they are brothers, but they are not from our tribes, and they have never been Muslim, and they do not have confidence that they would be warmly received by us.

That means that your people, white people from far away, had to come. You won our hearts when you asked our elders if you could have permission to live in our area. You stayed with us through that first "hungry season," even though it was hard for you to see some of our people grow weak and die. Now we have shared our milk with one another, and there is love and respect between us.

You said little, except about crop production, until the elders asked you to explain God's message. The elders wanted to hear from you again because your face was open. When the two orphaned boys needed new parents, the elders asked if you would take them. This was the moment that you became accepted by all the Yano on both sides of the river.

Please accept my handprint as a token of our love and affection.

Sheikh x, baptized 2007

Notes

Preface: An Invitation to a Journey

[1]All generalizations are inherently oversimplifications. Nevertheless, I'll use the term *Majority World* throughout this book to refer to the church in Latin America, Asia and Africa. I'll sometimes use terms like *non-Western church*, because that might be accurate too, but the term is one of negative identity. *Third World* and *Two-Thirds World* are still used, but most consider the terms passé. Others (and you will read this in some quotations) are talking about the church in the *Global North* versus the church in the *Global South* or the church in the *West* versus the church in the *East*, but these terms also have their limits. Unfortunately, none of the terms take into account the first-generation peoples and churches from the Majority World who now reside in North America. When I'm being this specific, I'll try to make the distinction plain.

[2]Although there are many differences between the churches and cultures of Canada and the United States, I use the term *North American church* throughout the book. Having said that, I should note that the Canadian church and culture have generally been more aware of global issues, more tolerant of diversity, less individualistic and assertive and more aware of the Majority World. Nevertheless, some of the attributes of dominant United States culture get assigned to Canadians, and Canadians may, unfortunately, suffer from guilt by association.

[3]Todd Johnson, interview with author, February 28, 2012.

[4]The book *Experiencing God* strongly affirms that God is at work in the world and the adventure of doing and knowing the will of God is about responding to God's initiating work. In the chapter "God Invites You to Join Him," the authors conclude with a prayer that summarizes their theme this way: "God, when You invite me to join You in Your work, I will respond immediately." Henry T. Blackaby and Claude V. King, *Experiencing God* (Nashville, Tenn.: Broadman and Holman, 1994), p. 129.

Introduction: Questions for the Journey

[1]Todd Johnson, interview with author, February 28, 2012. Todd is the director of the Center for Global Christianity at Gordon-Conwell Theological Seminary and coeditor (with Kenneth R. Ross) of the *Atlas of Global Christianity* (Edinburgh: Edinburgh University Press, 2009).

[2]Any number of books can help readers gain a broader understanding of the realities of the global church. Philip Jenkins's first edition of *The Next Christendom: The Coming of Global Christianity* led the way in 2002 with a broad introduction to the church around the world. Patrick Johnstone and Jason Mandryk's *Operation World: When We Pray God Works* has been guiding our understanding and prayers for decades. The *World Christian Encyclopedia* (David B. Barrett, George T. Kurian and Todd M. Johnson, eds.) and the *Atlas of Global Christianity* (Todd M. Johnson and Kenneth R. Ross, eds.) provide volumes of information that could take a lifetime to digest. And Patrick Johnstone's magnum opus, *The Future of the Global Church: History, Trends, and Possibilities* provides a thorough and detailed overview

of issues, statistics, trends and future forecasts. Mark Noll's *The New Shape of World Chris-tianity: How American Experience Reflects Global Faith* is a brilliant analysis, but it is gen-erally not for the church lay person who oversees a mission committee; Noll writes with an academic audience in mind. Also, it is descriptive of current realities but not insightful on what we in the Western world should do next. Similar things are true about the global-church works of Philip Jenkins (*The New Faces of Christianity: Believing the Bible in the Global South* and *God's Continent: Christianity, Islam, and Europe's Religious Crisis*), Miriam Adeney (*Kingdom Without Borders: The Untold Story of Global Christianity*) and Michael Pocock et al. (*The Changing Face of World Missions: Engaging Contemporary Issues and Trends*). Analysis provokes understanding, but might not be as helpful when an individual wonders where God might be leading or a church outreach committee asks questions about where to allocate finances or where to send short-term mission teams. Hence this book.

[3]From personal correspondence with Bill Taylor, November 29, 2011, referencing original interviews and research that he and Steve Hoke did in the revising and up-dating of the *Global Mission Handbook* (Downers Grove, Ill.: InterVarsity Press, 2009).

[4]A good resource here is Lesslie Newbigin's *Foolishness to the Greeks: The Gospel and Western Culture*, written by a retired lifetime missionary to India who realized upon his return to England that his own home country had become a mission field.

[5]Lesslie Newbigin again speaks to this theme in *The Gospel in a Pluralistic Society*.

[6]Timothy C. Tennent, *Invitation to World Missions: A Trinitarian Missiology for the Twenty-First Century* (Grand Rapids: Kregel, 2010), p. 31.

Part 1: Where Are We Now?

[1]The concept of understanding both the Word and the world comes from John Stott's book *Between Two Worlds* (Grand Rapids: Eerdmans, 1982). The book *Issues Facing Christians Today* (4th edition) by John Stott, John Wyatt and Roy McCloughry (Grand Rapids: Zondervan, 2006) serves as a great resource for understanding how and where Christians need to be involved.

[2]Todd Johnson, "Religious Demography and Global Christian Education" (presentation to the board of trustees, Wheaton College, Wheaton, Ill., February 10, 2012).

[3]Philip Jenkins, *The Next Christendom: the Coming of Global Christianity,* third ed. (New York: Oxford University Press, 2011), p. 3.

[4]A great resource on this topic is Douglas Jacobsen's *The World's Christians: Who They Are, Where They Are, and How They Got There* (Malden, Mass.: Wiley-Blackwell), 2011.

[5]Timothy C. Tennent, *Invitation to World Missions: A Trinitarian Missiology for the Twenty-First Century* (Grand Rapids: Kregel, 2010), p. 33.

[6]In *Civilization: The West and the Rest*, prolific British historian Niall Ferguson examines whether Western civilization, as we know it, is in decline. Ferguson quotes a member of the Chinese Academy of Social Sciences on what has contributed to the long dominance of the West. The Chinese intellectual said, "At first we thought it was your guns. Then we thought it was your political system, democracy. Then we said it was your economic system, capitalism. But for the last 20 years, we have known it was your religion." Fer-guson, *Civilization* (New York: Penguin Press, 2011); quoted in Jonathan Sacks, "Re-versing the Decay of London Undone," *The Wall Street Journal,* August 20, 2011, http://online.wsj.com/article/SB10001424053111903639404576516252066723110.html.

[7]Mark A. Noll, *The New Shape of World Christianity: How American Experience Reflects Global Faith* (Downers Grove, Ill.: IVP Academic, 2009), p. 42.

[8]Andrew Walls, "Demographics, Power and the Gospel in the 21st Century" (lecture, SIL International Conference and WBTI Convention, Waxhaw, N.C., June 6, 2002).

[9]Timothy Tennent, *Christianity at the Religious Roundtable* (Grand Rapids: Baker Academic, 2002), p. 26.

[10]Mark R. Gornik, *Word Made Global: Stories of African Christianity in New York City* (Grand Rapids: Eerdmans, 2011).

[11]Philip Jenkins, *God's Continent: Christianity, Islam, and Europe's Religious Crisis* (New York: Oxford University Press, 2007), especially chapter 4.

[12]Jenkins, *The Next Christendom*, pp. 131-33.

[13]Bill Taylor, "The Great Global Shift: Implications for Church and Mission" (seminar for mission leaders, Woodmen Valley Chapel, Colorado Springs, February 10, 2011).

[14]Zoher Abdoolcarim, "The Chindian Century," *Time*, November 21, 2011, pp. 28-35.

Utilitarian Historians

[1]Adapted from "History Lessons: Confessions of a Former Utilitarian," from my column in *Lausanne World Pulse,* September 20, 2002, www.lausanneworldpulse.com/world pulse/137.

[2]David J. Bosch, *Transforming Mission: Paradigm Shifts in Theology of Mission* (Maryknoll, N.Y.: Orbis Books, 1991), p. 389.

[3]Quoted in Norman Thomas, *Classic Texts in Mission and World Christianity* (Maryknoll, N.Y.: Orbis Books, 1995), p. 67.

Chapter 1: The State of the World

[1]Patrick Johnstone, *The Future of the Global Church: History, Trends and Possibilities* (Downers Grove, Ill.: InterVarsity Press, 2011), pp. 1-20.

[2]Philip Jenkins, *The Next Christendom: The Coming of Global Christianity* (New York: Oxford University Press, 2011), pp. 1-2.

[3]Mark Noll, *The New Shape of World Christianity: How American Experience Reflects Global Faith* (Downers Grove, Ill.: InterVarsity Press, 2009), pp. 20-21.

[4]Bill Dyrness, email message to author, July 22, 2011.

[5]The idea of autonomy for indigenous churches (i.e., local or national churches) refers to growth to the point of being *self-governing* (led by people from that culture), *self-funded* (not reliant on external funds), *self-propagating* (capable of planting more churches in their own culture or nation) and *self-theologizing* (able to interpret the Scriptures in a way that addresses their own cultural context). John Nevius proposed this idea in China in the late nineteenth century, but it was adopted first in Korea. But if this autonomy happens, will the North American church become globally irrelevant?

[6]The Great Migration usually refers to the movement of African Americans from the rural South to the more urban North in the mid-twentieth century.

[7]Todd Johnson, "Religious Demography and Global Christian Education" (presentation to the board of trustees, Wheaton College, Wheaton, Ill., February 10, 2012). Johnson also cites *Exceptional People: How Migration Shaped Our World and Will Define Our Future* (Princeton, N.J.: Princeton University Press, 2011). Ian Goldin and his coauthors point out in *Exceptional People* that never have so many people been on the move, and never have they been so unwelcome.

[8]An unreached people group is an identified ethnic-specific group that has no witness of the gospel and/or no self-reproducing church.

[9]*New York Times* Foreign Affairs columnist Thomas Friedman is a world recognized authority on globalization and world affairs. His bestselling books include *The Lexus and the Olive Tree: Understanding Globalization* (1999), *The World Is Flat* (2005), and *Hot, Flat and Crowded* (2008). In spite of Friedman's commitment to on-site visits, Christian leaders in India have told me that they think he relies too much on interviews with India's middle class (who are generally benefitting economically from globalization) rather than hearing the voices of the slum-dwellers and the impoverished.

[10]From a personal conversation with Zac Niringiye in Nairobi, Kenya, in December 1991.

[11]Noll, *New Shape*, pp. 33-35.

[12]Two helpful resources for better understanding global theology are Craig Ott and Harold Netland, eds., *Global Theology: Belief and Practice in an Era of World Christianity* (Grand Rapids: Baker Academic, 2006), and Timothy C. Tennent, *Theology in the Context of World Christianity: How the Global Church Is Influencing the Way We Think About and Discuss Theology* (Grand Rapids: Zondervan, 2007).

[13]Todd Johnson, "World Christian Trends" (lecture at Lausanne Bi-Annual International Leadership meeting, Budapest, Hungary, June 18-22, 2007).

[14]Jeffrey Gettleman, "Born in Unity, South Sudan is Torn Again," *The New York Times*, January 13, 2012, www.nytimes.com/2012/01/13/world/africa/south-sudan-massacres-follow-independence.html?pagewanted=all.

[15]Edward Wong, "An Ethnic War is Rekindled in Myanmar," *The New York Times*, January 20, 2012, http://video.nytimes.com/video/2012/01/19/world/asia/100000001296874/ethnic-war-rekindled-in-myanmar.html.

[16]Todd Johnson, at the Lausanne Bi-Annual International Leadership meeting in Budapest, Hungary, June 18-22, 2007, reported that "Christians are experiencing unprecedented suffering. Christians around the world are being persecuted for their faith. We estimate that over the entire history of Christianity, seventy million Christians have been killed for their faith. Over half of these were in the twentieth century alone, a century which historian Robert Conquest referred to as 'The Ravaged Century.'"

[17]Ibid., p. 145.

[18]Gordon College professor of biology Dr. Dorothy Boorse reported this on January 25, 2005, in a Gordon College Chapel report on the impact of the December 26, 2004, tsunami on the southeast coast of Sri Lanka.

[19]Dorothy Boorse, *Loving the Least of These: Addressing a Changing Environment* (Washington, D.C.: National Association of Evangelicals, 2011), www.nae.net/lovingthe leastofthese.

[20]Other Great Commission passages associated with Jesus' last commands to his disciples include Mark 16:15-18; Luke 24:45-49; John 20:21; and Acts 1:8.

A Book, a Movie, a Song

[1]Revised and adapted from my article "A Book, a Movie, a Song: Thoughts from Jenkins," *Lausanne World Pulse*, www.lausanneworldpulse.com/worldpulse/430.

[2]Quoted in Jenkins, *Next Christendom*, p. 1.

[3]Torli Krua, email message to author, July 15, 2011.

Chapter 2: An Appraisal of the North American Church

[1]Catherine A. Brekus and W. Clark Gilpin, eds., *American Christianities: A History of Dominance and Diversity* (Chapel Hill: University of North Carolina Press, 2011).

[2]Hwa Yung, "A Fresh Call for U.S. Missionaries: Americans Should Focus Less on 'Western Guilt' and More on Sharing the Gospel," *Christianity Today*, November 9, 2011, www.christianitytoday.com/ct/2011/november/fresh-call-for-missionaries.html. Quoted with permission from Bishop Yung.

[3]David Ro, email message to author, July 17, 2011.

[4]Steve Corbett and Brian Fikkert, *When Helping Hurts: How to Alleviate Poverty Without Hurting the Poor . . . and Yourself* (Chicago: Moody Press, 2009). William Easterly's *The White Man's Burden: Why the West's Efforts to Aid the Rest Have Done So Much Ill and So Little Good* (New York: Penguin Press, 2006) is a secular critique of Western foreign aid, but it raises questions that reflective givers need to ask.

[5]With respect to this optimism: some assume that the millennial generation has lost the spirit of optimism and that they are turning more pessimistic about the future. Anne Hong of InterVarsity Christian Fellowship and Ruth Hubbard of Wycliffe Bible Translators summarize their research with millennials in a presentation called "RESET with this Student Generation: Engaging Millennials in Missions." In this study, they assert that millennials are self-confident, "positive realists who think that they can make a difference." They report that 96 percent of millennials surveyed agreed with the statement "I believe I can do something great," and they conclude that today's college-age students "expect that they can make a difference in the world and are graduating from college ready to dive into being world-changers. They want to make an impact on the world and have the optimism and confidence to pull that off." Hong and Hubbard note that the downside of this confidence is their tendency towards brashness and arrogance, but they argue that their spirit of teachability may help temper this. Hong and Hubbard presented this material in a webinar sponsored by "Missio Nexus," July 8, 2011. It is available in audio format at http://sendu.wikispaces.com/file/view/Reset+with+this+Student+Generation+Engag ing+Millennials+in+Missions+download+webinar.pdf/276213862/Reset+with+this+ Student+Generation+Engaging+Millennials+in+Missions+download+webinar.pdf.

[6]Mark Noll, *The New Shape of World Christianity: How American Experience Reflects Global Faith* (Downers Grove, Ill.: IVP Academic, 2009), p. 91.

[7]Vishal Mangalwadi, *The Legacy of William Carey: A Model for the Transformation of a Culture* (Wheaton, Ill.: Crossway, 1999), p. 89.

[8]David Ro, email message to author, July 17, 2011.

[9]Development Associates International offer a Masters level course that I compiled titled Culture, Ethnicity, and Diversity. Using an inductive method, it takes leaders through issues from Scripture, history and current events and forces them to wrestle with where the role of ethnic identity fits in our Christian identity. Majority World students report regularly that because the course was compiled by an American who is willing to be self-critical concerning his personal and his culture's mistakes, it has helped them be more willing to examine their own ethnocentric tendencies. For more information, go to www.daintl.org or write to Development Associates International, P.O. Box 49278, Colorado Springs, CO 80949.

[10]Yung, "Fresh Call for U.S. Missionaries."

[11]John 14:6 with my elaboration.

[12]Timothy C. Tennent, *Invitation to World Missions: A Trinitarian Missiology for the Twenty-First Century* (Grand Rapids: Kregel, 2010), p. 25.

[13]Tim Dearborn, "Christ, the Church, and Other Religions," in Max Stackhouse, Tim Dearborn and Scott Paeth, eds., *The Church in a Global Era* (Grand Rapids: Eerdmans, 2000), p. 139.

[14]Karl Rahner asserted that people without a personal knowledge of or response to Jesus Christ were nevertheless saved (without knowing it) by Jesus' atoning sacrificial death and victorious resurrection. Thus the Hindu, Jew, Buddhist, Muslim and person of any other religion were saved "anonymously" by Jesus. For further reading on the ideas surrounding pluralism, see Dennis K. Okholm and Timothy R Phillips, eds., *Four Views on Salvation in a Pluralistic World* (Downers Grove, Ill.: InterVarsity Press, 1996); Paul F. Knitter, *No Other Name: A Critical Survey of Christian Attitudes Toward the World Religions* (Maryknoll, N.Y.: Orbis Books, 1985); Leo O'Donovan, ed., *A World of Grace: an Introduction to the Themes and Foundations of Karl Rahner's Theology* (Washington, D.C.: Georgetown University Press, 1995); and John Hick and Paul Knitter, eds., *The Myth of Christian Uniqueness: Towards a Pluralistic Theology of Religions* (Eugene, Ore.: Wipf and Stock, 2004).

[15]Robertson McQuilkin, *The Great Omission* (Waynesboro, Ga: Gabriel Resources, 1984), p. 42.

[16]Dearborn, "Christ, the Church, and Other Religions," p. 139.

[17]I recommend Timothy Tennent's book, *Christianity at the Religious Roundtable: Evangelicalism in Conversation with Hinduism, Buddhism, and Islam* (Grand Rapids: Baker Academic, 2002). In it, Tennent presents an excellent example of interacting with other faiths as an *engaged exclusivist*: someone who believes in the uniqueness of Christ but is willing to listen, learn and dialogue.

[18]Philip Jenkins, *The Next Christendom: The Coming of Global Christianity,* 3rd ed. (New York: Oxford University Press, 2011), p. 1.

[19]Cited by Ian Douglas, "Globalization and the Local Church," in *The Church in a Global Era,* ed. Max Stackhouse, Tim Dearborn and Scott Paeth (Grand Rapids: Eerdmans, 2000), p. 203.

[20]Ibid.

[21]Ibid., p. 210.

[22]Samuel P. Huntington, *The Clash of Civilizations and the Remaking of the World Order* (New York: Touchstone, 1996), p. 183.

[23]Benjamin Barber, *Jihad vs. McWorld: Terrorism's Challenge to Democracy* (New York: Random House, 1995).

[24]Tim Dearborn, "Conclusion," in *The Church in a Global Era,* ed. Max Stackhouse, Tim Dearborn and Scott Paeth (Grand Rapids: Eerdmans, 2000), p. 212, emphasis mine.

[25]Donald W. Shriver Jr., *An Ethic for Enemies: Forgiveness in Politics* (New York: Oxford University Press, 1995), p. 4.

[26]Harvey Cox, *Fire from Heaven: The Rise of Pentecostal Spirituality and the Reshaping of Religion in the Twenty-First Century* (Cambridge, Mass.: Da Capo Press, 1995), p. 63.

[27]Douglas, "Globalization and the Local Church," pp. 203-204.

[28]These statements from Rick Warren came in October 2003 in a generic email announcing the Saddleback "PEACE plan" (planting churches, equipping leaders, assisting the poor, caring for the sick, and educating the next generation). I know that Rick has softened some of his views since then, but his statements still resonate in the lives of pastors who hold to the centrality of the local church as the missionary sender. Unfortunately, these

same "we do it all" pastors tend to overlook (a) the implicit message in the "do it all" church plan that reflects a "from the West to the rest" view of global mission; (b) the valuable experience and wisdom gained by ministries who have served crossculturally for years; (c) the need for more listening to what is already going on in various locales; and (d) the sustainability of what these pastors propose (in other words, will our churches stay focused on one or two locales or will we lose interest and move on?).

[29]Todd M. Johnson, "'It Can Be Done'": The Impact of Modernity and Post-Modernity on the Global Mission Plans of Churches and Agencies," in *Between Past and Future: Evangelical Mission Entering the Twenty-First Century,* ed. Jonathan Bonk (Pasadena, Calif.: William Carey Library, 2003), p. 46.

[30]Douglas, "Globalization and the Local Church," pp. 204-5.

[31]Tim Dearborn, "Conclusion," in *The Church in a Global Era,* ed. Max Stackhouse, Tim Dearborn and Scott Paeth (Grand Rapids: Eerdmans, 2000), p. 212.

[32]See David Platt, *Radical: Taking Back Your Faith from the American Dream* (Colorado Springs: Multnomah, 2010).

[33]Neil Postman's famous book *Amusing Ourselves to Death* makes the point that our preoccupation with entertainment has dramatically affected our ability to think critically. Neil Postman, *Amusing Ourselves to Death: Public Discourse in the Age of Show Business,* rev. ed. (New York: Penguin, 2005).

[34]Patrick Johnstone, "The Next Forty Years for Global Mission," in *Global Passion,* ed. David Greenlee (Cumbria, U.K.: Authentic Publishing, 2003), p. 189.

[35]One agency raising support for indigenous leaders aired a commercial that featured a suburbanite waxing his car. He turned towards the camera and said, "I'm not just waxing my car; I'm planting churches in south Asia because I send $xx/month to [mission agency]." The implication—that all God asks of us related to global involvement is our money—reflects our materialistic culture. Biblically, he asks for our lives.

[36]From the introduction to Darrell L. Guder, ed., *Missional Church: A Vision for the Sending of the Church in North America* (Grand Rapids: Eerdmans, 1998), p. 6 (emphasis mine).

[37]These three questions are quoted from personal email correspondence from Doug Birdsall dated June 5, 2011. Although the manuscript of Doug's talk is not in print or online, the vast resource of the www.lausanne.org website includes many articles as well as global news that speak to these questions.

[38]Jairus Mutebe, personal correspondence to author, July 22, 2011.

[39]Richard Tiplady, personal correspondence to author, August 22, 2011.

[40]Andrew Walls, "Demographics, Power and the Gospel in the Twenty-First Century" (lecture, SIL International Conference and WBTI Convention, Waxhaw, N.C., June 6, 2002).

Chapter 3: An Appraisal of the Majority World Church

[1]In the children's book series The Chronicles of Narnia (New York, Collier Books, 1950), C. S. Lewis makes multiple references to Aslan, the Christ character, as being "not tame": *The Lion, the Witch, and the Wardrobe,* pp. 75-76, 180; *The Last Battle,* pp. 16, 72.

[2]Miriam Adeney. *Kingdom Without Borders: The Untold Story of Global Christianity* (Downers Grove, Ill.: InterVarsity Press, 2009), p. 109.

[3]Ibid, p. 110.

[4]Ibid, p. 241.

[5]Andrew Walls, "Demographics, Power and the Gospel in the Twenty-First Century" (lecture, SIL International Conference and WBTI Convention, Waxhaw, N.C., June 6, 2002).

[6]This figure was cited by a missionary at the conference; Operation World numbers Christians in Central African Republic at 76 percent (www.operationworld.org/cent).

[7]Patrick Johnstone, The Church Is Bigger Than You Think (Ross-shire, U.K.: Christian Focus Publishing, 2000), p. 25.

[8]I note later in the book that we in North America need to listen to the development of local, contextualized theologies before making judgments. But the rise of indigenous Christian movements led by people claiming authority that equals or supersedes the Bible does present a large theological challenge in terms of which groups and which leaders we should partner with. Timothy Tennent of Asbury Theological Seminary cites "constructing new theologies" as one of seven megatrends shaping twenty-first-century missions. He writes: "We now see the emergence of a Fourth Branch of Christianity. We can no longer conceptualize the world's Christian movement as belonging to Roman Catholic, Protestant, and Eastern Orthodox communions exclusively. The twenty-first century is characterized by enormous changes in Christian identity, which influence how the Christian message is understood and shared." He explains that this message is being shaped by new indigenous churches, what he calls "crypto Christians" and more. See Invitation to World Missions: A Trinitarian Missiology for the Twenty-First Century (Grand Rapids: Kregel, 2010), p. 37.

[9]Todd Johnson, "Religious Demography and Global Christian Education" (presentation to the board of trustees, Wheaton College, Wheaton, Ill., February 10, 2012), citing the World Christian Database.

[10]Adeney, Kingdom Without Borders, p. 50.

[11]An excellent resource here is J. Kwabena Asamoah-Gyadu's African Charismatics (Leiden, the Netherlands: Koniklijke Brill NV, 2005). The same author has an informative introduction to the issues of prosperity theology online at www.christianity today.com/globalconversation/november2009/index.html.

[12]Prosperity teaching in parts of West Africa has been so attractive to people that a movement of Muslim miracle-workers and healers has risen up offering the same benefits as Jesus, only from Allah. Sometimes these groups are called Chrislam or operate under the name NASFAT, for Nasr Allah al-Fatih Society of Nigeria (translation: there is no help except from Allah). For more information, see the NASFAT website, www.nasfat.org, or Marloes Johnson, "Learning to be Redeemed: Chrislam's Healing School in Lagos" (presentation, ECAS conference, Uppsala, Sweden, June 15-18, 2011), www.nai.uu.se/ecas-4/panels/101-120/panel-115/Marloes-Janson-full -paper.pdf.

[13]Adeney, Kingdom Without Borders, pp. 249-50.

Part 2: Moving Forward

[1]Fareed Zakaria, The Post-American World: Release 2.0 (New York: W. W. Norton, 2011). Also speaking to the diminishing dominance of the United States in the world and the greater need to work in partnership with other nations are: Thomas Friedman and Michael Mandelbaum, That Used to Be Us: How America Fell Behind in the World It Invented and How We Can Come Back (New York: Farrar, Straus, and Giroux, 2011) as well as

Lionel Barber's essay, "The end of US Hegemony," *Financial Times,* September 5, 2011, www.ft.com/cms/s/0/f6acf1a6-d54d-11e0-bd7e-00144feab49a.html#axzz1X6Wts8zi. Analysts cite many reasons in their analysis of why North American influence in general and the United States influence in particular have declined, but most the most noteworthy reasons include: (1) the growth of other economies (most notably China and India); (2) the lingering bad feelings in the world towards the West regarding the Iraq and Afghan wars; (3) the staggering growth of national debt in the West and in the United States; and (4) American pride.

[2]Zakaria, *Post-American World,* p. 1.

[3]"Global Mission Comission Consultation 2011," World Evangelical Alliance Mission Commission *Agora* newsletter (December 2011), p. 3, describing the WEA MC Consultation in Stuttgart, Germany in November 2011.

[4]This section is a modification of what I wrote in "What About the Poor," *Vital Ministry* (May/June 1998, p. 58).

[5]For more information or to order copies of the pledge, email Evangelicals for Social Action at esa@esa-online.org or visit www.evangelicalsforsocialaction.org.

Chapter 4: Biblical Continuity

[1]Doug Birdsall, personal correspondence to author, July 21, 2011.

[2]Mary Lederleitner, personal correspondence with author, August 11, 2011. See also Lederleitner, *Cross-Cultural Partnerships: Navigating the Complexities of Money and Mission* (Downers Grove, Ill.: InterVarsity Press, 2010).

[3]Andrew Walls, *The Cross-Cultural Process in Christian History* (Maryknoll, N.Y.: Orbis, 2002), p. 81.

[4]These eight bullets from John 3:16 are built off of a sermon I preach on that text. The sermon is available online at http://vimeo.com/32084427.

Chapter 5: A Posture of Humility

[1]Lamin Sanneh, *Translating the Message: The Missionary Impact on Culture* (Maryknoll, N.Y.: Orbis, 1989).

[2]The biblical principle of Jesus' incarnation as the Word of God made flesh (Jn 1:1, 14) provides the Christian theological foundation for wanting to put the Bible as the printed word of God into the local languages so that everyone can understand that God wants to be known by them. Sanneh points out that "translatability" is one of the greatest contrasts of Christian mission versus Muslim (Sanneh, *Translating the Message,* pp. 211-14). The Koran in Arabic is untranslatable because it is a replication of tablets that exist in heaven. Arabic is Allah's only language—to the point that offering prayers in your mother tongue could make a Muslim an outcast (ibid., p. 213).

[3]I learned this phrase "reflective practitioners" from Bill Taylor of the World Evangelical Alliance Mission Commission.

[4]Isaiah Lawon, personal correspondence with author, July 16, 2011.

[5]Adele Calhoun, personal correspondence with author, July 16, 2011.

[6]Cassells Morrell, personal correspondence with author, July 18, 2011.

[7]Richard Tiplady, personal correspondence with author, August 22, 2011.

[8]Duane Elmer, *Cross-Cultural Servanthood: Serving the World in Christlike Humility* (Downers Grove, Ill.: InterVarsity Press, 2006).

[9]Another helpful book is David Livermore, *Serving with Eyes Wide Open: Doing Short-Term Mission with Cultural Intelligence* (Grand Rapids: Baker, 2006).

[10]Hwa Yung, "A Fresh Call for U.S. Missionaries: Americans Should Focus Less on 'Western Guilt' and More on Sharing the Gospel," *Christianity Today,* November 2011, www.christianitytoday.com/ct/2011/november/fresh-call-for-missionaries.html.

Chapter 6: Purposeful Reciprocity

[1]Affy Adeleye, personal correspondence with author, July 25, 2011.

[2]Quoted in Philip Jenkins, *The Next Christendom: The Coming of Global Christianity,* 3rd ed. (New York: Oxford University Press, 2011), p. 1.

[3]Ibid., p. 3.

[4]Dr. Samuel Escobar used this phrase in the paper he presented to the 1999 gathering of the Mission Commission of the World Evangelical Fellowship (now World Evangelical Alliance) to describe the Western obsession with plans and numbers and strategies rather than focusing on relationships. The phrase provoked such dialogue that it appears more than a dozen times in the compendium of this event. See Samuel Escobar, "Evangelical Missiology: Peering Into the Future," in *Global Missiology for the 21st Century: The Iguassu Dialogue,* ed. William D. Taylor (Grand Rapids: Baker Academic, 2000), p. 109.

[5]Paul R. Gupta, "What the Global Church Wants the West to Know About Partnership" (plenary address, COSIM conference, Orlando, Fla., June 20-22, 2005, emphasis added).

[6]Ian Douglas, "Globalization and the Local Church," in *The Church in a Global Era,* ed. Max Stackhouse, Tim Dearborn and Scott Paeth (Grand Rapids: Eerdmans, 2000), p. 207.

[7]The *Round Trip* video curriculum is devoted to developing two-way, give-and-receive relationships across cultures. It features the young adult ministries from a church in North Carolina partnering with a church from Kenya, with each group joining the other in service in the two locations. The curriculum accurately depicts some of the challenges of crossing cultures, building trust and learning to receive from each other.

[8]Isaiah Lawon, personal correspondence, July 16, 2011.

[9]Adapted from my article "The Problem of Utilitarian Friendships," *Lausanne World Pulse,* www.lausanneworldpulse.com/worldpulse/564.

Changing Dynamics in Global Relationships

[1]The material that follows is adapted from Jimmy Lee's email newsletter dated August 5, 2011, "Lessons From the Global Church." The group Jimmy Lee leads is Create Possible (www.createpossible.com) and this specific essay is online at http://margaretfeinberg .com/index.php?option=com_wordpress&p=3986&Itemid=5.

[2]T. J. Addington, "Moving Strategy from Black and White to the Color World," a seminar presented at the RESET Conference, Phoenix, Ariz., September 30, 2011. Summary available at http://wernermischke.org/2011/10/14/nine-critical-shifts-for-world-missions-by-t-j-addington/.

[3]Steve Moore, "Mission at the Crossroads: Towards a Strategic Narrative for North American Missions," *eXcelerate* 3, 2011, pp. 4-7, www.themissionexchange.org/down loads/eXcelerate_2011.pdf.

Chapter 7: Sacrifice—Not Just Generosity

[1]Jimmy Lee, "What I Learned from Poverty (Lessons Learned from the Dominican Republic," Create Possible email, October 14, 2011.

[2]Gregg Easterbrook, *The Progress Paradox: How Life Gets Better as People Feel Worse* (New York: Random House, 2004), p. 80.

[3]Ibid., p. 182.

[4]Ibid., pp. 182-85.

[5]Related to the American dream, a brother from a Majority world country rebuked me gently when I pointed out the propensity of the poorer world to go after prosperity teaching. He replied, "You don't see yourselves as going after prosperity because you already have it and you're asking God to give you more."

[6]One of the more interesting conclusions of Easterbrook's book, given that it is not written from any particular religious framework, is that the best way to combat the depression that accompanies rampant individualism and runaway consumerism is to get past our own concerns and go serve someone less economically fortunate. As Jesus said, "Whoever loses their life for my sake will find it" (Mt 10:39).

[7]Kay Warren's book *Dangerous Surrender* tells her story of two bouts with cancer and how she turned that suffering into concern for people with HIV/AIDS in Rwanda.

[8]Read the biographies of historical missionaries like Mary Slessor in Calabar (now part of Nigeria) or Amy Carmichael in India, and you'll discover that their efforts in rescuing children from suffering and sexual abuse was, in part, a work of God to redeem the difficult childhood of these missionaries. See James Buchan, *The Expendable Mary Slessor* (Norwich, U.K.: St. Andrew Press, 1980), and Elisabeth Elliot, *A Chance to Die: the Life and Legacy of Amy Carmichael* (Old Tappan, N.J.: Revell, 1987).

Chapter 8: Partnership Equality

[1]Duane Elmer, foreword to Mary T. Lederleitner, *Cross-Cultural Partnerships: Navigating the Complexities of Money and Mission* (Downers Grove, Ill.: InterVarsity Press, 2010), p. 11.

[2]Joe Handley, personal correspondence with author, August 11, 2011.

[3]Richard Tiplady, personal correspondence with author, August 22, 2011.

[4]Ron Blue, personal correspondence with author, August 11, 2011.

[5]Bill Taylor, "The Great Global Shift: Implications for Church and Mission" (workshop, Woodmen Valley Chapel, Colorado Springs, February 10, 2011, emphasis added).

[6]Robert Morrison, quoted in J. Oswald Sanders, *Spiritual Leadership* (Chicago: Moody Press, 1994), p. 62.

[7]Hwa Yung, "A Fresh Call for U.S. Missionaries: Americans Should Focus Less on 'Western Guilt' and More on Sharing the Gospel," *Christianity Today*, November 2011, http://www.christianitytoday.com/ct/2011/november/fresh-call-for-missionaries.html.

[8]Steve Corbett and Brian Fikkert, *When Helping Hurts: How to Alleviate Poverty Without Hurting the Poor . . . and Yourself* (Chicago: Moody, 2009), p. 115.

[9]Ibid., pp. 115-19.

[10]Andrew Walls, "Demographics, Power and the Gospel in the Twenty-First Century" (lecture, SIL International Conference and WBTI Convention, Waxhaw, N.C., June 6, 2002).

[11]I refer you here again to Mary Lederleitner's *Cross-Cultural Partnerships* because it is the best book specifically addressing the "complexities of money and mission." Jonathan Bonk's *Mi$$ion$ and Money: Affluence as a Western Missionary Problem* (Maryknoll, N.Y.: Orbis, 1991) strongly rebukes the insensitivity of Western missionaries to the relational impact of the economic divide between themselves and Majority World leaders, but Mary Lederleitner offers more constructive solutions.

[12]Todd Johnson, "Religious Demography and Global Christian Education" (presentation to the board of trustees, Wheaton College, Wheaton, Ill., February 10, 2012).

[13]Bruce Camp, "A Survey of the Local Church's Involvement in Global/Local Outreach," in Jonathan Bonk, ed., *Between Past and Future: Evangelical Mission Entering the Twenty-first Century* (Pasadena, Calif.: William Carey Library, 2003), p. 242.

Chapter 9: Listening to Our Non-Western Brothers and Sisters

[1]Zac Niringiye, personal correspondence with author, July 16, 2011.

[2]On a visit to a Taliban-controlled area of Afghanistan several years ago, we asked our hosts if we could meet any Afghan followers of Christ. Our hosts replied, "No, because if you did meet them, the Taliban would be at that location within the day, and that Afghan person would be dead."

[3]Andrew Walls, "Demographics, Power and the Gospel in the Twenty-First Century" (lecture, SIL International Conference and WBTI Convention, Waxhaw, N.C., June 6, 2002).

[4]Robby Muhumuza, personal correspondence with author, July 16, 2011.

[5]Soong-Chan Rah, *The Next Evangelicalism: Freeing the Church from Western Cultural Captivity* (Downers Grove, Ill.: InterVarsity Press, 2009).

[6]Ibid., pp. 85-86.

[7]Ibid., p. 162.

[8]Rah in *The Next Evangelicalism* dedicates an entire chapter to "Suffering and Celebration: Learning From the African-American and Native American Communities," pp. 143-63.

[9]Miriam Adeney, *Kingdom Without Borders: The Untold Story of Global Christianity* (Downers Grove, Ill.: InterVarsity Press, 2009), pp. 257-58.

[10]Philip Jenkins, *The New Faces of Christianity: Believing the Bible in the Global South* (New York: Oxford University Press, 2006).

[11]Mark A. Noll, *The New Shape of World Christianity: How American Experience Reflects Global Faith* (Downers Grove, Ill.: IVP Academic, 2009), p. 190.

[12] Walls, "Demographics, Power and the Gospel."

[13]Arnold and Gerri Polk, personal correspondence with author, August 6, 2011.

[14]Jairus Mutebe, personal correspondence with author, July 22, 2011.

[15]Adeney, *Kingdom Without Borders,* pp. 187-201.

[16]Prabhat Narjinary, personal correspondence with author, July 22, 2011.

[17]Adeney, *Kingdom Without Borders,* pp. 167-69.

[18]Ibid., p. 179.

[19]The comments from Reuben Ezemadu are condensed from personal correspondence with Bill Taylor, November 29, 2011, referencing original interviews and research that he and Steve Hoke did in the revising and updating of the *Global Mission Handbook* (Downers Grove, Ill.: InterVarsity Press, 2009).

[20]The story of Bautista and his village is the focus of Mark Ritchie's book, *Spirit of the Rainforest: A Yanomamo Shaman's Story* (Wauconda, Ill.: Island Lake Press, 2000).

[21]Adeney, *Kingdom Without Borders,* p. 152.

[22]Niyi Gbade, personal conversation with author, September 10, 2011.

[23]James Magara, "Missions: Then and Now" (presentation, African Inland Mission, Nairobi, Kenya, January 16, 2004).

[24]"The African Planter: An Interview with Oscar Muriu," *Leadership Journal,* Spring 2007 www.christianitytoday.com/le/2007/spring/3.96.html.

[25]From personal correspondence with Bill Taylor, November 29, 2011.

[26]Sam Thomas, personal correspondence with author, July 19, 2011. Thomas also cautions North American churches and ministries to make sure that the leaders they invest in are living and leading with integrity and accountability locally. He states that those who are good at telling heartrending stories can often convince North Americans to give, but "I personally feel that giving money into the hands of people without local credibility is a harm for the ministry in India and also damaging to the church."

[27]Orality refers to ministry with people classified as oral learners. These people are often illiterate, but even if literate, they "learn and remember through stories, proverbs, drama, songs and chants. They are just as smart as literates but have not learned the skills of literacy. Their memories are better and they can easily reproduce what they hear." "Orality," Call2all website, copyright Church Insight (accessed July 12, 2012), http://call2all.org/Groups/1000014486/call2All/Strategic_Themes/Orality/Orality.aspx.

[28]Phil Chinn, personal correspondence with author, July 22, 2011.

[29]Bobby Bose, personal correspondence with author, July 15, 2011.

[30]Important short-term mission note here: repeating short-term missions at the same location is one of the best ways to build trust, mutuality and longer-term relationships

[31]Bobby Bose, personal correspondence with author, July 15, 2011.

[32]Eva Lee, personal correspondence with author, July 16, 2011.

[33]Cassells Morrell, personal correspondence with author, July 18, 2011.

[34]Isaiah Lawon, personal correspondence with author, July 16, 2011.

[35]Durwood Snead, personal correspondence with author, July 16, 2011.

[36]Jairus Mutebe, personal correspondence with author, July 22, 2011.

[37]Hwa Yung, "A Fresh Call for U.S. Missionaries: Americans Should Focus Less on 'Western Guilt' and More on Sharing the Gospel," *Christianity Today*, November 2011, www.christianitytoday.com/ct/2011/november/fresh-call-for-missionaries.html.

[38]Gary A. Haugen, *Good News About Injustice* (Downers Grove, Ill.: InterVarsity Press), pp. 37-39.

Chapter 10: United Together—So That the World Might Know

[1]"Global Mission Commission Consultation 2011," *Agora*, newsletter describing the World Evangelical Alliance Mission Commission Consultation in Stuttgart, Germany in November 2011.

[2]Timothy C. Tennent, *Invitation to World Missions: A Trinitarian Missiology for the Twenty-First Century* (Grand Rapids: Kregel, 2010), p. 47.

[3]Todd Johnson, "Religious Demography and Global Christian Education" (presentation to the board of trustees, Wheaton College, Wheaton, Ill., February 10, 2012).

[4]Max Stackhouse, Tim Dearborn and Scott Paeth, eds., *The Local Church in a Global Era: Reflections for a New Century* (Grand Rapids: Eerdmans, 2000), p. 213.

[5]Miriam Adeney, *Kingdom Without Borders: The Untold Story of Global Christianity* (Downers Grove, Ill.: InterVarsity Press, 2009), p. 281.

[6]Some of this material appeared in my "Business Can Heal the Community," *Lausanne World Pulse*, 2003, www.lausanneworldpulse.com/worldpulse/334.

[7]You can find the Integra website at http://integra.sk.

Conclusion: Responding to the Invitation

[1]Paul R. Gupta, "What the Global Church Wants the West to Know About Partnership" (plenary address, COSIM Conference, Orlando, Fla., June 20-22, 2005).

[2]Lesslie Newbigin, The Gospel in a Pluralist Society (Grand Rapids: Eerdmans, 1989), p. 101.

[3]Doug Birdsall, from his presentation at the morning plenary session (untitled) at Orlando 2011, the joint conference of the Mission America Coalition and the Lausanne Movement (Orlando, Fla., April 6, 2011).

[4]Tom Lin, from his presentation at the evening plenary session (untitled) at Orlando 2011, the joint conference of the Mission America Coalition and the Lausanne Movement (Orlando, Fla., April 5, 2011).

[5]Birdsall, morning plenary session at Orlando 2011.